Leonardo's Notebook

At the time Leonardo's mules were schlepping the notebooks around Italy, the pages were valuable only to their author. Today they are among the most precious things on the planet. The notebooks, the core obsession of Leonardo's life, are what place him among the giants of science, not specific discoveries he made or new inventions he created.

So what are they, exactly?

We call them "notebooks," but they are not bound like a typical notebook. Mostly they are loose sheets of paper casually gathered together and wrapped with different fabrics. Some pages are large. Others are only two or three inches square; these must be from the tiny blank notebooks he always kept tied to his belt.

Leonardo went out of his way to make the notebooks difficult for any other person to read—tremendously out of his way. The main roadblock is his famous mirror-image script. His tiny writing goes backward, reading from right to left. The drawings aren't backward, just the words.

What was he thinking?

LEONARDO DA VINCI

KATHLEEN KRULL

ILLUSTRATED BY **BORIS KULIKOV**

PUFFIN BOOKS
An Imprint of Penguin Group (USA)

PUFFIN BOOKS
Published by the Penguin Group
Penguin Group (USA) LLC
375 Hudson Street
New York, New York 10014

USA * Canada * UK * Ireland * Australia
New Zealand * India * South Africa * China

penguin.com
A Penguin Random House Company

First published in the United States of America by Viking,
a division of Penguin Young Readers Group, 2005
Published by Puffin Books, a division of Penguin Young Readers Group, 2008

THE LIBRARY OF CONGRESS HAS CATALOGED THE VIKING EDITION AS FOLLOWS:
Krull, Kathleen.
Giants of science : Leonardo da Vinci / by Kathleen Krull ; illustrated by Boris Kulikov.
p. cm.—(Giants of science)
Europe, 1452 : so many things unknown!—The outsider—The desire to know is natural—Nothing
but full toilets—Lying on a feather mattress—The universe stands open—Miserable mortals, open
your eyes!—The fabulous notebooks—The notebooks, part 2—I want to work miracles!—I will
continue—What happened next?—Leonardo's notebooks and where they are now.
Includes bibliographical references and index.
ISBN: 978-0-670-05920-1 (hc)
[1. Leonardo, da Vinci, 1452–1519—Juvenile literature. 2. Scientists—Italy—Biography—Juvenile
literature. 3. Science, Renaissance—Juvenile literature. 4. Leonardo, da Vinci, 1452–1519—
Influence—Juvenile literature. 5. Leonardo, da Vinci, 1452–1519—Notebooks, sketchbooks, etc.—
Juvenile literature.]
I. Kulikov, Boris, date. II. Title. III. Giants of science (Viking Press)
Q143.L5 K78 2005 509'.2—dc22 2005007244

Puffin Books ISBN 978-0-14-240821-6

Designed by Jim Hoover

Printed in the United States of America

9 10

For Jane O'Connor — K.K.

Acknowledgments
For help with research, the author thanks
Robert Burnham and Patricia Laughlin,
Patricia Daniels, Dr. Lawrence M. Principe,
Susan Cohen, Gary Brewer, Dr. Helen Foster James
and Bob James, Sheila Cole, Janet Pascal, Gery Greer,
and Bob Ruddick.

CONTENTS

INTRODUCTION   8

CHAPTER ONE
"So Many Things Unknown!"   11

CHAPTER TWO
The Outsider   17

CHAPTER THREE
"The Desire to Know Is Natural"   23

CHAPTER FOUR
"Nothing but Full Privies"   35

CHAPTER FIVE
"Lying on a Feather Mattress"   40

CHAPTER SIX
"The Universe Stands Open"   50

CHAPTER SEVEN
Citizen of the World   60

CHAPTER EIGHT
The Fabulous Notebooks   68

CHAPTER NINE
The Fabulous Notebooks, Part 2   74

CHAPTER TEN
"I Have Wasted My Hours"   93

CHAPTER ELEVEN
"I Will Continue"   101

CHAPTER TWELVE
What Happened Next?   105

LEONARDO'S NOTEBOOKS
AND WHERE THEY ARE NOW   115

BIBLIOGRAPHY   120

INDEX   125

INTRODUCTION

"If I have seen further [than other people]
it is by standing upon the shoulders of giants."

—Isaac Newton, 1675

*W*HERE DO SCIENTISTS' brilliant ideas
and discoveries come from?

Well, nobody lives in a vacuum, and ideas don't
come out of nowhere. Even Isaac Newton (a giant of
science if ever there was one) depended on what great
thinkers before him had figured out in order to "see
further," to make discoveries of his own.

People hear the name Leonardo da Vinci, and they
think "artistic genius of the Renaissance." And sure,
he created the *Mona Lisa* and *The Last Supper*, two
of the world's most famous paintings.

Yet for thirty years—the whole last half of his

life—he spent most of his time doing research in fields ranging from astronomy to anatomy, zoology to geology, and botany to paleontology.

"Scientist" wasn't even a word Leonardo would have known—people didn't start using the term until the early nineteenth century. (He might have called himself a natural philosopher—someone who wants to make sense of the natural world.) But he would have known the Latin word *scientia*, which means "knowledge"—knowledge that explains the universe and the principles that make it work. Leonardo was *very* interested in *scientia*.

Yet, in books about scientists, Leonardo isn't always included. Perhaps that's because, in the history of science, Leonardo is like a bridge. He stands right between the medieval view of the world and the modern view based on observation and experimentation. He looks backward to a time when nature seemed illogical, magical. He looks ahead to a time when nature is viewed as operating by rules and laws that can be discovered.

Leonardo did indeed "see further" than anyone of his era. But whose "shoulders" did he stand on? And, in turn, did his work, his discoveries, inspire other scientists?

CHAPTER ONE

"So Many Things Unknown!"

EUROPE IN THE Middle Ages—first of all, there were no books. No printed books, that is. Just manuscripts in Latin, tediously copied by hand for the rich. Peasants had never seen one. Most people couldn't read or write anyway.

There were no bathrooms. Hardly anyone knew what soap or underwear was. The poor ate with their fingers; utensils were for the rich. Most adults had no more than a few teeth in their heads.

Almost half of all children died before they were a year old. Women, on average, could expect to live only until age twenty-four. That's because so many didn't survive childbirth.

In the countryside, the poorest peasants lived in extreme poverty and filth, ten to twenty people to a damp hut. They slept on the floor, their farm animals—as well as rats—beside them. After a bad harvest, when a famine would sweep through, people starved to death.

In cities, streets served as toilets, and piles of excrement were left to mold until the next rain. Every few decades came a mysterious plague called the Black Death for the hideous black blisters it inflicted. The epidemic of 1348, which killed one out of every three people in Europe, was ascribed by many doctors to the rare placement in the sky of three planets.

Doctors varied wildly in training, and progress in medicine was sluggish. There were physicians with degrees from famous universities. Still, the books they studied had been written more than a thousand years earlier. Other "doctors" had little or no schooling; barbers sometimes performed surgery. And if a limb had to be amputated, pouring boiling oil onto the wound was the method used to stop bleeding. A urine flask was the universal symbol for physicians; they spent more time examining urine than anything else.

Doctors knew how to set broken bones. But the surefire cure for nosebleed? Pig manure.

Ten green lizards, cooked slowly in olive oil, were believed to heal an open wound. One medicine was made from earthworms washed in wine and donkey's urine; another called for a horn of a unicorn. Gout, a painful swelling of the joints, was treated by placing a sapphire ring on a certain finger of the patient. Blood-sucking leeches, applied when the planets were in alignment, could fix many ailments. More common was simply slicing open the skin, trying not to sever an artery, to allow the release of "bad" blood.

People's lives were short and violent. The rate of accidental death was high; the murder rate was twice as high. Many rulers were tyrants—some homicidal. Wars were common. No country, or even city, was stable. Women were viewed as vain—the devil's decoy. And if they stood out in any suspicious way, they might be tried for witchcraft—and burned.

The all-powerful Catholic Church was a beacon of light and learning in Europe in the Middle Ages. But non-believers were often brutally persecuted.

In ancient Greece and Rome, in China, and in

Arab countries, scientists had discovered much about astronomy, medicine, mathematics, and more. Islamic scholars translated the work of ancient Greek scientists into Arabic, keeping their discoveries alive, adding their own ideas to them. But in Europe, much of this body of knowledge was lost for a long time—centuries in fact.

"Sciences" in medieval times did include astronomy and mathematics, but it was still an age when people believed in magic. So "pseudosciences" were taught as well—the study of angels; physiognomy, the link between a person's character and what he or she looks like; astrology, the belief that the planets influence human behavior; and alchemy, the "study" of how to make gold out of other metals.

Learned men argued whether or not angels supplied the force that kept the planets in motion. And they counted only seven planets—of which Earth was not one. Instead, Earth occupied the center of the universe, with other astronomical bodies like the sun revolving around it.

But a great wave was splashing across Europe, changing how people thought in some very fundamental ways. The result was a new confidence in human achievement, what was possible to do in one's lifetime here on Earth. This led to an explosion of new information and exchange of new ideas. All this coincided with a wonderful rediscovery of the ancient knowledge that had been lost.

Atop the wave of change was Leonardo da Vinci. He was born at the right time in the right place: in 1452 and in Italy. Because by then, it was officially the Renaissance, a glowing burst of fireworks in art, architecture, literature, and science. And nowhere was the Renaissance spirit brighter than in Florence, Italy.

As Leonardo grew up, he looked around him. He had an amazing flair for looking, like no one else in history before him.

"So many things unknown!" he wrote one day. But he wanted—and was determined—to find answers for himself. His method was to start questioning everything. His method was scientific.

CHAPTER TWO

The Outsider

THE YEAR WAS 1452. The place was the hilltop town of Vinci, in Tuscany, Italy. Towns don't get much smaller. Vinci was a sleepy village of about fifty small buildings.

Piero da Vinci, at twenty-six years old, was an up-and-coming notary. That was his family trade—recording and certifying legal documents. Success made the family respectable middle-class landowners. Piero was so ambitious that he already had eleven convents as steady clients. His work kept him mostly in Florence, only a day's journey by horseback. The independent city-state of Florence was the opposite of Vinci—a teeming intellectual and artistic center in northern Italy.

Piero seems to have been a player, a man-about-town. One of his relationships was with Caterina, a local peasant woman. Marriage was never the goal; we don't even know her last name. But she had a baby: Leonardo. Being born illegitimate would set up roadblocks for Leonardo all his life.

Children with unwed parents were common enough. The nobility and peasantry took them in stride, but for people in the middle class, people like Piero, these children were bastards—embarrassing, even hated. To be illegitimate was like having a bright red tattoo on your forehead—you were an affront to morality, a mistake better off erased.

A few months after his son was born, Piero married someone else—a fifteen-year-old girl. In all, Leonardo was going to have four stepmothers to deal with, plus at least fifteen half brothers and sisters.

So he was born an outsider. Even as a baby he had no clear home. No one knows where he spent his first few years. He probably lived with Caterina for at least a year and a half so that she could nurse him. A few years later, she married and moved to another village. Without Leonardo. After this, every time he saw her, on religious holidays, she would be nursing a new baby—she had five more children.

When he was four, a powerful storm bombarded the area around Vinci, with flooding, fierce winds, and immense destruction. "Against the fury [of water], no man can prevail," Leonardo later wrote. "An act of God" was how most people explained such a storm, but Leonardo came to think otherwise. He developed a lifelong interest in storms and water, which he saw as natural forces. For the rest of his life, he was obsessed with the study of water—how it behaved, and especially how it might be controlled.

By age five Leonardo was living with his grandparents. His grandmother was sixty-four, his grandfather almost eighty-five. Truly ancient!

From what is known, Leonardo's sounds like the loneliest of childhoods. Children in the 1400s were not coddled or entertained. They were thought of as miniature adults. The only one to show interest in Leonardo was his uncle, Francesco. Sixteen years older than his nephew, he farmed the family's land. He coaxed it into producing olives, wheat, and grapes.

Francesco was a bit of a scientist-farmer, brimming with practical knowledge, always experimenting with different crops. Leonardo spent many hours helping his uncle with farm chores and taking long walks in the hills. The boy observed all creatures with equal fascination, even the lizards and worms in the vineyard. He learned the names of plants and herbs and all about variations in weather. Francesco loved nature and seemed to pass this on to his nephew.

The area around Vinci is one of the most gorgeous spots in the world—both then and now. Streams and waterfalls intersect fairy-tale forests and faraway mountains with castles perched on top. Fields of glowing wheat melt into groves of silvery olive trees. Rolling hills in every shade of green, all dotted with the red-tiled roofs of farmhouses, are bathed in misty light that shimmers and glows.

There are stories that young Leonardo carried a drawing pad with him at all times—that he drew constantly and sculpted models out of clay. Most people had little access to pencils or expensive paper, but he had them in his house because of the family's business. It was said that he collected everything—flowers, leaves, pieces of wood, animals.

The natural world was Leonardo's first laboratory. In the hills around Vinci, he spent hours observing— the movement of birds' wings in flight, how a frog's legs allowed it to leap so far, water running in a river—which in turn led to a greater understanding of the forces of nature and to a fascination with sciences like biology, botany, and geology.

His formal schooling was minimal. His grandparents might have hired private teachers or had him taught by the parish priest. He learned basic math using Roman numerals and an abacus, and how to read and write in Italian, the everyday tongue of the people. It didn't occur to anyone to teach him Latin, the international language of scholars.

Leonardo was four when a major breakthrough in communication occurred. For the first time, a book was printed, following Johannes Gutenberg's invention of movable type in 1456. The first printed book in Europe was, of course, a Bible. And soon, books— all kinds of books—were easily available.

Did Leonardo have any books as a child? None of his own, certainly. His family might have owned one or two. As a member of a Christian family, young Leonardo would have heard Bible readings and seen paintings in the local church. All his life, the more he learned about the workings of the world, the more respect he had for the mind of God. "The Creator does not make anything superfluous or defective," he marveled.

Still, he could be critical of church practices and didn't become a regular churchgoer, following his beliefs in his own way instead. He seldom spoke about religion or miracles: "I do not attempt to write or give information of those things . . . which cannot be proved by an instance of nature."

Because of his illegitimacy, he was not allowed to attend one of the famous universities in Italy. No one seemed to expect anything respectable of this boy. No one bothered to try to correct his left-handedness, at a time when this trait was forcibly discouraged and even considered evil by some.

All his life, Leonardo had to teach himself. Sometimes he was bitter about this, but as he grew older he also took pride in being what people called him: "unlettered." By then, he had realized that what was being taught as fact wasn't necessarily right.

CHAPTER THREE

"The Desire to Know Is Natural"

*B*EING ILLEGITIMATE WAS a lasting black mark. Leonardo was barred by law from most respectable professions as well as from advanced schooling. Piero's guild of notaries, for example, refused entry to the illegitimate, as well as to criminals.

Leonardo's choices in life were limited: either join the army (where many illegitimate boys ended up) or get his hands dirty taking up a trade.

His father clearly felt responsible for Leonardo's future. When the boy was twelve or thirteen, Piero took him along on one of his trips to the pulsing big city of Florence. One of five independent city-states in what is now Italy, Florence was the cutting-edge center of the art world.

Perhaps the boy had already impressed people with his talent for art. And artists didn't necessarily *have* to be respectable. Piero might have considered a career in art the most viable option for his son.

Piero did have connections. He got his son apprenticed as a studio boy to Andrea del Verrocchio, the leading Florentine painter and sculptor of his day. This was one of the luckiest breaks of Leonardo's whole life.

Verrocchio's workshop was like a buzzing little art factory. A storefront, opening onto the street, enticed customers with its wares—paintings and sculptures, musical instruments, helmets, bells, and baskets. Spartan living quarters for the artists were on top of or behind the storefront, with beds of straw on the floor.

In exchange for working, Leonardo was fed and sheltered and paid a small amount. Verrocchio was now his legal guardian. He even had the right to beat him, though there is no evidence that he did.

Artists at that time had to be practical and versatile, to make things people really used. Leonardo plunged into an array of projects, such as painting altarpieces and panels, making large sculptures in marble and bronze, copying coats of arms, decorating pottery, designing tools for surgery. The young artists in the studio worked mostly in teams, finishing one another's work, rarely signing their names. Art was about craft, not ego.

As a boy straight out of the country, the teenage Leonardo must have been a little gawky at first. But he soaked everything up, drew energy from his new environment, and simply blossomed.

As it happened, Florence was perhaps the most percolating place for anyone to be in the 1460s. The ruler, Lorenzo "the Magnificent" de' Medici, tried to encourage an atmosphere of commerce and culture. Other Italian cities, such as Bologna and Pisa, also nurtured new ideas. But merchants from all over loved Florence for its central location. After recovering from a deadly attack of the plague, its population was booming again, approaching 100,000 hustling and bustling people.

More than many other cities, Florence had people who were rich and well educated. For decades it had been controlled by the Medici family, who were wealthy from banking. Although often cruel and corrupt, the Medici did nourish the arts. Verrocchio's workshop, in fact, was generously supported by orders from the powerful Medici—for sculptures, candelabra, banners and other decorations, and even their tombs.

A new boy (at the time, artists' apprentices were always boys) would start out sweeping the floor, running errands, cleaning paintbrushes, and heating up varnish or glue. As he learned the basics of drawing, his special talents would reveal themselves. He would graduate to crafting paintbrushes from animal hair, stretching canvases, mixing the paints from scratch, and applying gold leaf to backgrounds.

The apprentice would learn about the use of color, how to lay down the first coats of tempera (an egg-based paint), how to transfer a drawing to another surface, how to paint directly onto walls, and how to carve stone. He might be allowed to finish whole sections of paintings depending on whether he was good at landscapes, clothes, or faces. He would have to work some twelve hours a day, every day of the week except Sunday, every week of the year.

Leonardo was continually practicing his drawing. There was a lot to learn. In the Middle Ages, images in paintings had appeared flat, limited to two dimensions. But in 1413, the architect and artist Filippo Brunelleschi worked out the mathematical principles of linear perspective. Now paintings could give the illusion of depth. A young artist like Leonardo would need to study mathematics in order to portray nature as it actually appeared, in three-dimensional space.

The workshop was like another laboratory for Leonardo, after the natural world of his early childhood. Its spirit was almost as much scientific as artistic, with observations and experiments leading to new techniques. An apprentice would be always experimenting with potions—oil of cypress with water to make an amber-colored paint, saliva to keep pens wet. One job was to prepare wood panels for painting; in later life, Leonardo revealed his recipe as a lengthy process using twice-distilled turpentine, arsenic, boiled linseed oil, and human urine.

The first big project Leonardo probably helped see through to completion was a two-ton giant bronze ball. It was for the city's famous cathedral—to go atop its dome, designed by Brunelleschi. Every man and boy in the workshop was called upon to help. The final hoisting of the ball into place was a huge celebration that Leonardo certainly attended—along with the whole shouting city.

Being an artist could clearly bring sparkling acclaim.

It also brought approval from his father.

One day Piero stopped by the workshop. He had a plain wooden shield he needed painted as a favor to someone. Leonardo took the job and went all out. He decided the picture on a shield must be frightening, so he collected lizards, bats, crickets, snakes, insects. Then he dissected them. He arranged the most interesting body parts into the scariest possible monster, spitting fire. He painted the beast on the shield, which he displayed in a corner of a dark room, and invited his father in for a dramatic unveiling.

Piero was actually frightened at first, then delighted. He took it away and picked up a cheap shield (decorated with a simple heart pierced by an arrow) to give to his friend. Did Piero keep his son's shield? No. He sold it for a nice sum.

Verrocchio encouraged his apprentices to dissect small dead animals as a way to learn to portray anatomy. This was something easy, if unusual, for Leonardo to do. In fact, in the study of anatomy at that time, artists were as knowledgeable as anyone, even medical students.

Verrocchio required his artists to depict the

human form with complete accuracy, which meant they were expected to study how the body was constructed. Instead of working from the imagination, they had to draw live models. They could also make plaster casts of body parts, both their own or those of corpses.

It seems Verrocchio was one of those inspiring teachers who change lives. He was like a one-man university himself. He knew everything about art, plus he was an experimenter and innovator. He encouraged his shop to break new ground in the arts, not just to repeat the past. To think big.

"The painter must strive to be universal," Leonardo would write later. From Verrocchio he learned that an artist should be capable of rendering anything in nature.

Leonardo was definitely a quick learner. Word spread fast that the new apprentice could draw and paint like an angel. Verrocchio delegated more and more work to him. The boy's confidence must have soared.

Life at Verrocchio's was not all work and no play. The shop was a gathering place for artistic and literary young men. Artists from other shops would stop by, as would travelers passing through Florence.

They exchanged recipes for paints, modeled for one another, and drank wine. Ideas ricocheted about all things—philosophy, nature, science, and the latest books.

Leonardo's early education in scientific matters came from chatting with visitors to Verrocchio's workshop. Collectors in Turkey and Greece who had libraries of ancient manuscripts—including the philosophy of Plato and Aristotle—were now selling them to collectors in Florence. Every time a manuscript from ancient times was translated, a buzz would go around the city.

Leonardo and his friends also enjoyed playing the role of artistic rebels, out to shock respectable citizens with frivolous behavior. Nothing too outrageous, as the laws were strict and penalties often severe. Mainly pranks—Leonardo was famous for the stink balls he created out of fish remains or decomposing animals.

Leonardo seemed to fit right in. Perhaps it was the only time in his life when this was true. He had friends from all walks of life, respectable and otherwise. A good singer, he also excelled at the viol, a stringed instrument played with a bow. He invented party tricks, like throwing red wine into a cup of boiling oil to make colorful flames erupt. Witty at parties, he told good riddles and funny stories (most of which haven't stood the test of time).

Even accounts that rarely describe appearances *always* call Leonardo handsome. He was probably asked to pose for other artists. While long flowing robes were the fashion of the day, he wore rose-colored tunics that stopped short of his knee. His hair and beard were carefully combed and curled. In an age when bathing was optional, he was fanatic about being clean. He hated getting any paint under his fingernails.

The Medici fostered a party atmosphere around Florence, with jousting tournaments, carnivals, feasting, and other pleasurable amusements. Having fun was more important than anything. Leonardo, besides helping to provide decorations via the workshop, was reportedly an enthusiastic partygoer.

But he was also a private person. He spent time alone, thinking. He still took long walks in the hills nearby, carrying pen and paper everywhere in his sack. Even then he did not believe in walking for mere relaxation—it was an opportunity to "exercise" his eyes. A true artist never stopped perfecting observation skills.

His mind was open to beauty and to its opposite. In slums and hospitals, he looked for people he considered grotesque or deformed, furthering his study of anatomy. He would follow unusual-looking people for days, sketching.

"The desire to know is natural to good men," Leonardo wrote later, endlessly curious about more and more subjects.

Meanwhile, Florence was becoming famous—or notorious, depending on your point of view—for its openness to new, even controversial, ideas.

Once Gutenberg invented movable type, books began to be printed at a rapid rate. Because there were so many more books around, many more people learned to read. Now, ancient works of literature were printed and bound into books that people (wealthy ones) could actually buy. For any one new book on the market, thirty buyers were fighting to buy it and read it.

The universities cultivated independent thought. Paolo Toscanelli, the most famous astronomer of the time, taught in Florence. An engaging teacher, Toscanelli may have been the first one to guide Leonardo toward science. Independently wealthy, he was able to devote his life to science, especially to studying the paths of comets. He knew as much about celestial phenomena and the characteristics of Earth as anyone in his day. A geographer as well, Toscanelli once wrote a letter encouraging explorer Christopher Columbus in his belief that the lands of the East could be reached by sailing west around the globe.

Toscanelli's good friend, the artist-writer-engineer Leon Battista Alberti, had even more impact on Leonardo. One of the great intellectuals of the time, he advocated the application of science to art—artists should know about geometry, optics, the mathematical rules of perspective, and as much about human anatomy as possible. When Leonardo read Alberti's statement, "The painter ought to possess all the forms of knowledge useful to his art," he was electrified.

Alberti was one of the first men of the Renaissance to urge humans to strive, to excel. This was a revolutionary idea at the time—that humans had great, untapped potential. The self *did* matter—one person could make a difference. There was great optimism about the future.

Leonardo deliberately sought out older, more educated men. Everything interested him—"all the forms of knowledge" that Alberti spoke of. He may have sat in on lectures at the university, may have approached professors to ask questions. It's possible that while working on a project, he boarded with Lorenzo "the Magnificent," the Medici then in power. There he would have been exposed to the movers and shakers in Italy, people almost as smart as he was.

By 1472, at age twenty, Leonardo was no longer an apprentice. He was entered as an official member of the Florentine painters' guild, one of the two dozen trade associations representing various careers. The painters' guild of St. Luke had split off from the guild of doctors and druggists (who sold the materials for paints).

He was a full citizen now and could set up his own shop. Yet he remained as Verrocchio's assistant, perfecting his skills. He stayed twelve to thirteen years more with his teacher, which was longer than normal for most apprentices. Later in his life, when stressed, he would return to hang out here. It was a happy, sheltered place for him.

But not as sheltered as he thought. At some point during his years with Verrocchio, Leonardo was being spied upon.

CHAPTER FOUR

"Nothing but Full Privies"

WHEN LEONARDO WAS twenty-four, something awful happened. He was arrested.

The Medici family schemed and plotted to keep Florence under its thumb. One way was to encourage citizens to inform on one another. Anonymously, people could make accusations about illegal or immoral behavior by simply writing and slipping the allegations into boxes called *buchi della Verità* ("mouths of Truth"), which were prominently displayed at churches.

The idea was to keep people in line, or at least on

edge. Anybody could accuse anyone of anything, with or without proof. That was enough to start a police investigation. So the system was an easy way to get someone you didn't like into trouble with the authorities.

The dreaded Office of the Night had only one function. It was to check out accusations of homo-sexual sex, which was interpreted as being against the teachings of the Bible and considered a serious crime. During its seventy-year reign over Florence, the Office of the Night investigated 17,000 accused men, convicting some 3,000. The penalty tended to be a crushing fine, which was mild compared to punish-ments inflicted elsewhere or at other times in Florence—public whipping, exile, castration, indefi-nite imprisonment, or even death by burning. Part of the fine went as a reward to the informer, and the rest went to pay the expenses of the six Officers of the Night.

This was the office that summoned Leonardo in 1476. Someone had anonymously accused four men— Leonardo, a goldsmith, a tailor, and someone related to Lorenzo de' Medici—of having sex with a male prostitute.

It was a nasty turn of events. Leonardo and his three companions had to appear in a court of justice. They may have been imprisoned in a cell overnight or longer. Torture and other incentives were commonly used to get people to confess. But the four men didn't; they declared their innocence. Still, for some reason, another hearing was called.

Leonardo must have been frightened. Normally, parents would help out in such a crisis. But Leonardo probably dreaded his father's reaction to this particular charge. Piero, whose notary business was thriving, needed to maintain his respectability. Artists and intellectuals may have been more tolerant of homosexuality, but not the average citizen. Possibly, Leonardo feared a showdown between his father and himself, or considered arrest equal to failure in his father's eyes.

The anxiety and uncertainty lasted for over two months, through a second hearing—and then a third. In the end, the Office of the Night dismissed the charges. There were no signed statements from witnesses, nor apparently any firm evidence. It's possible Leonardo was simply a bystander in a plot to make trouble for the Medici.

Even though he escaped punishment, the artist was left bruised. The public embarrassment alone would have pained an intensely private person like Leonardo. And this particular case probably attracted greater publicity because of the Medici connection.

Historians disagree about Leonardo's sex life, or whether he even had one. But most think he was probably homosexual. He left no record of any relationship with a woman, not even a friendship. Various writings show he shared the common male attitude of his time: women were less intelligent than men and full of "useless chatter." He described the act of procreation as "repulsive."

Homosexuality was illegal. Other cities prosecuted vigorously, but the authorities in Florence generally fostered a don't-ask-don't-tell policy. In fact, homosexuality there was so widespread that the German word for homosexual at the time was *Florenzer*. But being discreet was crucial. The scandal of an investigation and conviction could ruin one's reputation. And career.

For the rest of his life, Leonardo would feel persecuted, whether or not he had reason to. He despised being the subject of gossip. As to the idea of prison, he declared, "It is better to die than to lose one's free-dom." Two of his very first designs were for devices to escape from a locked cell.

After the humiliating arrest, he structured his life so that he was free to be himself, isolated as much as possible from nosy neighbors. Was it then that his mistrust of and disdain for other people began? "How many people there are," he once wrote, "who could be described as mere channels for food," producing "nothing but full privies," or toilets.

CHAPTER FIVE

"Lying on a Feather Mattress"

I T MAY SEEM that Leonardo was taking the slow route to becoming a scientist. Investigating the natural world, that took time and earned him no money. As much as he dreaded what he called being a "slave" for money, he did need it. So his investigations into scientific subjects were, for the time being, hobbies.

Over the next several years, he buried himself in his work, attempting to strike out on his own as an independent master. He had his own studio and lived alone, but visited Verrocchio often. He probably had pets—he loved animals.

He was known around Florence as the young star artist from Verrocchio's studio, a strikingly attractive man who seemed good at . . . everything. He was funny and intelligent, capable of discussing any topic. He had a fine singing voice and was considered the best improviser in verse of his time—a sort of Renaissance rap artist. He was even good at sports, known for great strength, particularly as an excellent horseman.

But Leonardo did have flaws.

For someone with no other means of support, he was careless about business dealings. When he finally got commissions to do work, sometimes he followed through—and sometimes he didn't. With his first solo commission, in 1478, for a painting in a chapel, he got only as far as a sketch before quitting.

Later, in 1481, he was hired to create *The Adoration of the Magi*, a painting for the friars of a Florentine monastery. This was never finished, either.

In fact, Leonardo left behind more sketches and plans—and less finished work—than probably any other artist in history. How to explain this apparent lack of follow-through? Art lovers throughout history have mourned Leonardo's lack of productivity. The number of paintings (finished or unfinished) that we know to be his is only *thirteen*.

Is it possible for someone to be *too* smart? For him, a man with so many talents and so many passions, focusing on one idea or project may have been tricky. In a case, perhaps, of Renaissance attention deficit disorder, he always wanted to be on to the next thing.

Painting was not a means of self-expression for Leonardo—he thought of each painting as "a thing of the mind," a set of problems a brain could gnaw on. He was always much more interested in the conception of a project—figuring out how it would look or be constructed—than the completion of it. Sometimes he was so ambitious in his designs that he imagined ways of doing projects that were technically impossible, that no human could pull off.

It sounds like he could be bristly to work with. He turned down commissions from people he didn't like, or who had the nerve to treat him in a demeaning way. He hated being given orders or being rushed. Deadlines and contracts were obviously not sacred to him.

Perhaps Leonardo daydreamed instead of focusing. The artist did always have a hard time getting out of bed in the morning. "Lying on a feather mattress or quilt will not bring you renown," he once wrote, as if scolding himself. One of his early designs was for a personal alarm clock cleverly powered by water.

Or maybe he was growing ambivalent about fame, realizing it could bring attention of an unwanted kind.

Anyway, he was busy—busy reading, another pastime that earned him nothing. But it was important to him to fill in the craters in his education. Luckily, he was talented at teaching himself. He made notes of books he needed to read. By the time he was twenty-nine, in 1481, some 40,000 titles were in print.

Florence was home to a flourishing library, protecting thousands of rare items collected by the Medici. Like all libraries at that time, it wasn't open to the public, but Leonardo could have made the right connections to gain entry, reading what had been translated into Italian.

He also made notes of scholars to meet—an astronomer and geographer, a doctor, several mathematicians, a scholar of Greek. He must have discovered the fact that most experts adore talking about their area of expertise.

He was currently most interested in animal and plant biology, human organs, and the principles of flight. A beloved subject of Florentine art was the Greek myth of Icarus, the boy who flew too near the sun with wings of wax and feathers. Leonardo was obsessed with the possibility of flying. A long-standing legend is that Leonardo, who cherished animals, would often buy caged birds at the market just to set them free. First, though, he would study them—even his earliest paintings of angels showed that he was using real bird wings as models. He studied birds' wings and tails, how their feathers were arranged. Then he watched and made notes describing how birds flew up and down, changing direction, soaring, gliding, and coming in for a landing without breaking their legs.

His papers from this time show his deep interest in classical learning. He knew about Archimedes, the mathematician who was considered the greatest scientist of ancient Greece. Among other accomplishments, Archimedes had worked out the principles of the lever, using notions that were two thousand years ahead of his time.

Leonardo was also getting acquainted with the work of Plato, the Greek philosopher who linked knowledge with virtue.

Plato's best-known student, Aristotle, was Leonardo's favorite ancient Greek. Aristotle had studied biology, physics, medicine, and other fields, seeking grand truths that explained the natural world. He developed a system of reasoning to arrive at truths, known as Aristotelian logic. A classic example is: Every Greek is a person. Every person is mortal. Therefore every Greek is mortal.

Aristotle's lectures, collected by his followers, made up a kind of one-man encyclopedia of some 150 volumes. Arab scholars had preserved the great man's works, which were now available in translation in Florence. In his own thinking, Leonardo started out as a disciple of Aristotle, then later began questioning his ideas and branching out. Aristotle believed, for example, that the moon produced its own light, while Leonardo came to think (correctly) that the moon's light was reflected sunlight. Leonardo never followed anyone blindly.

Leonardo also showed an acquaintance with the controversial work of Roger Bacon, the brilliant thirteenth-century English philosopher, scientist, and monk. Bacon's work, too, formed a universal encyclo-pedia of knowledge. He was another Aristotle fan, and way ahead of his time in scientific thinking—he advocated controlled experiments, the testing of ideas. This was a whole new concept, one that must have had profound influence on Leonardo's own thinking. Aristotle and Plato found experiments pointless compared to the beauty of logic and mathematics.

Besides studying, Leonardo also had practical problems on his mind. With the city-states of Italy at war so much of the time, he was constantly sketching machines of warfare—this seemed a better bet for making money than painting. People who could design weapons were highly employable, and even though he personally hated war, designing machines fascinated him. On paper, he created innumerable tanks, crossbows, cannons, bombs, and guns.

At the same time, he was sketching machines that were powered by water or that could be used to transport water. He drew submarines, a snorkel, a machine for pumping water from underground, machines that would pump water through buildings, and a device that measured moisture in the air.

Having "graduated" from Verrocchio's studio, Leonardo didn't want to be thought of as a mere artist, an artisan. His role model was Giotto, a Florentine painter-architect who had died a century earlier, but who impressed Leonardo as a well-rounded innovator. "Giotto was not satisfied with imitating the works of his master," Leonardo wrote. Leonardo wanted to be an original. He was much more interested in inventing and designing. An engineer-architect—now, that was a worthy goal. Plus, it would leave plenty of free time to study nature.

To further his studies, Leonardo needed time and support. He needed a protector who would cocoon him from the stress of earning money, a friend in a high place to ward off the prying eyes of the police. He needed a patron.

Unfortunately, it was becoming clear that Lorenzo de' Medici was not going to be that patron. When the most important man in Florence wanted a job done, he sent it to artists who were Leonardo's rivals. Extremely well educated, Lorenzo may have looked down on the "unlettered" artist, who didn't know Latin, much less Greek.

Or perhaps Lorenzo just had a blind spot as far as recognizing Leonardo's talent. In 1481, the pope asked him to send the best artists to work on the new Sistine Chapel. Leonardo didn't make the cut. This seemed a bad omen for his future in Florence.

In fact, it was almost as big an embarrassment as his arrest. As he approached thirty, Leonardo's only fame so far came from being named in a sordid court case.

It was time to get out of Florence.

CHAPTER SIX

"The Universe Stands Open"

THE YEAR 1482, when he was thirty years old, was a turning point in Leonardo's life.

He left Florence to make a fresh start in the wealthy city-state of Milan, two hundred miles to the north. It was there that he began keeping notebooks that explored all areas of the natural world.

He knew no one in Milan, a big city with twice as many people as Florence. The city was not as famous for art as it was for advances in science and learning. It was one of the centers for Italian book publishing. Milan also boasted a university with ninety distinguished professors, the University of Pavia, and one of the best libraries in all of Italy— a dream place to study.

Milan's ruler, Duke Ludovico Sforza, while a corrupt dictator, was nurturing a hospitable atmosphere for thinkers and artists. With fewer artists than Florence, there should be less competition for his talents, Leonardo hoped.

Leonardo drafted a now-famous job application to Duke Sforza.

"I can invent an infinite variety of machines," he stated, going way out on a limb to elaborate. He said he could build portable bridges; knew the techniques of constructing bombardments and making cannons; could build ships, armored vehicles, catapults, and other war machines; and could execute sculpture in marble, bronze, and clay. Most cleverly, he promised to build the immense bronze horse that Sforza wanted as a memorial to his father. "In painting," he ended blandly, "I can do as well as anyone else." His modesty about painting seems odd. But Leonardo was playing up the talents he knew would be valued most by a war-mongering duke.

He probably never sent the letter—a good thing,

as it was mostly bluff. But the letter revealed something about his current mood. Producing art was not Leonardo's main goal now; he wanted more. His painting was merely useful as a skill he could fall back on if other ventures didn't pan out.

Once in Milan, he rented a room and studio space from the Preda family—six brothers, all artists. His best friend was Donato Bramante, a fellow artist and a future designer of St. Peter's Basilica in Rome. Both men were interested in mathematics, and were followers of artist-author Leon Battista Alberti.

Leonardo also met frequently with Fazio Cardan—a professor of medicine and mathematics—and his family. Cardan had edited a famous textbook on optics, written by a thirteenth-century English archbishop. During long talks with Cardan, Leonardo learned what was known at that time about how the eye worked. The eye was called the "window of the soul," a concept that Leonardo took further, to identify it as the central way men could understand "the infinite works of nature." While others of his day believed the lens was the most important part of the eye, Leonardo was more interested in the retina and how an image is formed there when light strikes it.

Eventually, by being in the right place at the right time, he did succeed in entering the service of Ludovico Sforza. The duke clearly valued Leonardo, who served him for years as principal military engineer and also as an architect. His job was to be versatile—produce a painting or sculpture here, design a courtyard there, create new and deadly weaponry, entertain the court with his music one day, invent an improved olive press another day.

During these early years in Milan, disaster struck—another epidemic of the Black Death. The disease hit fast and furiously. More than ten thousand Milanese died. Corpses, swarming with rats, were left for days in town squares, awaiting burial. Possibly it was at this time that Leonardo concocted the rose water perfume he liked to wear, to cover the ever-present "evil smell" of death.

Leonardo, who somehow avoided getting sick, tried to understand more about the disease. Most people assumed the plague was simply bad fortune destined by the stars, or God's punishment for wickedness. Many Christians accused Jews of deliberately spreading the disease; an outbreak was often an excuse to step up persecution of the Jews.

Everyone knew the plague was contagious, but no one knew how to stop it. Although unaware of its cause—bites from infected rats and fleas—Leonardo rightly connected unsanitary living conditions with the disease. His response to the plague was typically ambitious. He drew up a plan to reorganize all of Milan. He wanted to make the city cleaner, healthier. Milan's streets were narrow, filthy, and overcrowded, intersected by canals from which frogs chirped nightly, but that also carried human waste. The drinking water was contaminated. When people took baths at all, they shared water at public bathhouses.

For Leonardo, the plague must have caused two years of great anxiety, grief at losing friends, and daily trauma. He soothed himself by constructing, on paper, his version of an ideal city. Clean and efficient, it would stretch both horizontally and vertically—to two levels. The rich nobility would live above, in open spaces with parks. (Leonardo was a man of his time in believing that the rich were better people than the poor.) The streets would be very wide, to allow for fresh air and sunlight. The lower, darker level was for the less fortunate, with homes for the shopkeepers and—significantly, reflecting their status in society—artisans.

His detailed plans provided for plumbing, drainage, transportation of animals and people, and waste disposal. He had devices to wash the streets, and chimneys that blew smoke high above roofs. To stop people from using dark street corners as toilets, he planned bathrooms whose ceilings had many holes for ventilation, and even designed toilets with swiveling seats.

He wrote out rules for good health: "Visits to the toilet should not be postponed. Eat only when hungry and let light fare suffice. Chew your food well. . . ."

And speaking of food, in addition to the other things that set him apart—and unlike just about every other fifteenth-century Italian—Leonardo was a vegetarian. (He believed that any creatures that moved felt pain.) He despised people who shot birds for sport. He thought that men who ate meat were walking tombs and that someday people would no more murder animals than they would kill other people. In an era known for rich foods and serious feasting, he stuck to minestrone soup, peas cooked in almond milk, green salads, fruit, wine, and bread.

After the Black Death had passed, the city didn't rebuild itself according to Leonardo's designs. He had no authority to put his ideas into practice, and it's not clear whether he even showed them to anyone. But Milan, freed from overwhelming death, *was* reenergized. Now Sforza and other officials poured money into constructing new buildings, remodeling old ones, and staging festivals and masques—much activity to keep Leonardo busy.

But not too busy. Leonardo also spent a great deal of time alone, either walking around the countryside or sitting all day in his studio. "If you are alone, you will be your own man," he once wrote. He never stopped observing, questioning, or reading. When most people considered comets and eclipses and similar phenomena alarming messages from beyond, Leonardo considered them events in nature. He even devised devices for studying a solar eclipse without eye damage.

For years he had been in the habit of writing down his ideas—doodles, observations, to-do lists— on stray scraps of precious paper. But now, in Milan, he got serious, especially about his interest in the natural world, and began his famous series of note-books.

Into these notebooks went all of his nature draw-ings, experiments, and theories about the world. He worked by candlelight, sometimes all through the night. With the intense curiosity of a small child, he asked questions about *everything*: What is milk? What causes tickling or vomiting or sneezing? Why is the sky blue? What kind of machine could fly? Where do tears come from? Why do we urinate and defecate? What exactly is drunkenness, madness, dreaming...?

These are not diaries, though every once in a while a morsel of personal detail slips through. The notebooks are professional, businesslike (for him). Leonardo listed the subjects that were of most pas-sionate interest to him—and came up with twenty. They included botany, optics, hydraulics, astronomy, geology, physics, and anatomy—he was doing the first of his amazing drawings of the human body. The notebooks show the birth and development of Leonardo the natural philosopher, Leonardo the scientist.

Leonardo did not compartmentalize his interests. To him, all knowledge was related. What he could learn in one field would help shed light on others. This attitude allowed him to cross-fertilize ideas in unusually creative ways. He thought of architecture, for example, as related to human anatomy. Buildings resembled bodies; the more he could learn about anatomy, the better an architect, or "building doctor," he would be.

In his notebooks, Leonardo's goal was the direct study of nature. "Nothing can be found in nature that is not part of science," he wrote. "Science is the captain, and practice the soldiers."

He decided early on that firsthand experience— using the five senses—was the means of discovering scientific truths. Experience to confirm theories was absolutely crucial: "The greatest deception men suffer is from their own opinions." And direct experience was certainly more important than reading about others' experience: "The grandest of all books, I mean the Universe, stands open before our eyes."

Leonardo valued knowing what great minds before him had thought, hence his ongoing self-education. But he didn't necessarily accept their views. He called some scholars "stupid fools" for relying solely on the works of other men, for not thinking for themselves—investigating, questioning.

The people who impressed him most were those inventors who discovered ways to control nature.

In these new notebooks, Leonardo was thinking about science, and he was really thinking big. Inspired by Aristotle perhaps, he planned eventually to publish them as a grand encyclopedia of scientific knowledge, a system for understanding everything. His research and writing would occupy him for the next thirty-seven years. Like many of his projects, this one was never finished.

But what he did accomplish was beyond magnificent. The result was thirteen thousand pages that scholars have divided into ten assortments.

Leonardo was out to question everything. Like others during the Renaissance, he was discovering he could think for himself: "Anyone who argues by referring to authority is not using his mind but rather his memory." He was taking the first steps—baby steps—toward the methods of modern science.

CHAPTER SEVEN

Citizen of the World

*T*HE HEAVENS—or what we call outer space—were one of Leonardo's obsessions in his notebooks, and his next job for Duke Sforza appealed to this interest.

In 1490, the duke invited all of Italy's elite to Milan for a great spectacle designed by Leonardo: the Feast of Paradise. The theme was to be astrology. Leonardo's task was to create the party's climax, a pageant called *The Masque of the Planets*. Perhaps it seems surprising to us that someone with such a critical mind accepted some of the ideas of astrology. But he did. Everyone did. However, Leonardo did scorn astrologers who made money by preying on foolish people. (He thought they should be castrated.) The visual possibilities of the astrological theme excited him to outdo himself. Hundreds of workers carried out his plans for the masque.

At the stroke of midnight, after the dancing and feasting, the duke stopped the music. He raised the curtain on Leonardo's latest creation: a gigantic revolving stage shaped like an enormous half-egg.

Inside floated models of what were then considered the seven planets—Mercury, Venus, Mars, Jupiter, Saturn, the sun, and the moon. Earth was not considered a planet, and Uranus, Neptune, and Pluto hadn't been discovered yet.

Each planet revolved in its orbit, along with the signs of the zodiac illuminated by torches behind colored glass. Other torches flamed bright yellow, representing the stars. The effect was outrageous.

At age thirty-eight, Leonardo had arrived. By now he had been promoted to what he considered the ideal job: *ingeniarius ducalis*, engineer-architect to Duke Sforza of Milan.

Never had he enjoyed such financial stability. The duke gave him an entire wing of an old palace, opening onto the cathedral square, as a comfortable home and workshop. He also gave him precious land for a vineyard. Leonardo could finally think about building his own house. For now he supported a household of a dozen or so students, servants, and friends. His workshop was a hive of activity, buzzing with apprentices, with Leonardo as a gentle father figure.

Best of all, he had plenty of spare time and the free

run of the excellent library at the university. He had access to scholars and librarians. Some professors became his friends.

He was far from wealthy, but now he did have money to *buy* books. He owned more than most scholars, including Ptolemy's *Cosmography*. (It was Ptolemy who, in the second century, cemented the theory—still held in Leonardo's lifetime—that Earth was the center of the universe.)

Around this time, Leonardo informally adopted a ten-year-old boy he nicknamed Salai, or Demon. No one else liked the boy—he stole, lied, and constantly embarrassed Leonardo, who wrote, "He eats as much as two boys and causes as much trouble as four." He might have started out as a servant—peasant children entered service at ten. But to Leonardo he also served as a model, a pupil and assistant, and a companion— almost a son, and someone to indulge. Whatever his faults, Salai stayed with him for almost thirty years.

During his time in Milan, Leonardo was laboring on one of his most famous masterpieces, *The Last Supper*, painted on the wall of the dining room in a monastery. He would paint for days without eating or drinking. Or he might show up to study the mural for many hours, make one brush stroke, then take off. Two years passed. Eventually he finished, but alas, his experimental use of oil paints on the dry plaster wall was unsound. The mural began deteriorating during his own lifetime.

Leonardo also devoted years of intense study to the duke's favorite project, the twenty-four-foot-high bronze horse. Leonardo even dissected horses to study their anatomy. He became probably the world's foremost expert on horses. And he was fascinated by the technological difficulty of creating a horse that big. But the bronze creature never got built.

We know that by now he was wrapped up in scientific investigations.

He became lifelong friends with Luca Pacioli, author of the first printed algebra book. A mathematician, Franciscan monk, and fellow disciple of Alberti, Pacioli was one of the most respected intellectuals in Italy and an important influence on Leonardo. Leonardo sought tutoring in math—never his best subject—from Pacioli. Math was changing at its most basic level. People were switching from the limited system of Roman numerals (no zero, no fractions) to the Arabic system, which we still use today.

Pacioli also helped with Leonardo's study of the Greeks—Archimedes, and also Euclid, whose ancient works in geometry were available in Italy. It was Euclid who had worked out the principles that the whole is equal to the sum of its parts, and that a straight line is the shortest distance between two points.

Leonardo repaid Pacioli's help many times over. He later illustrated the monk's most celebrated work, *Divina Proportione*, which built on the five complex geometric shapes in nature as defined by Plato.

Leonardo preferred to keep his scientific work secret. Pacioli was one of the few people Leonardo trusted enough to show his notebooks. Work on the meticulously illustrated notebooks was an ongoing nightly activity. Leonardo was beginning to organize them by themes—the first was to be optics, his theories about the eye and how we see.

There was just so much to be learned, so much to discover. "Obstacles cannot crush me," he proclaimed with resolve. "He who is fixed to a star does not change his mind."

He listed over 170 books he had read so far, from a textbook on surgery and a pamphlet about urine, to

Pliny's *Natural History*, Aristotle's *Physica*, and various mathematical treatises. He was always on the lookout for new books: one on proportion, another on waterworks, a new translation of Aristotle on the heavens. He searched for years for a copy of Archimedes' treatise *On Floating Bodies*. Archimedes remained the one ancient Greek he always respected; the others he came to disagree with.

So starving was he for knowledge that, when he was past forty, he started teaching himself Latin, the scholarly language. This was so he could finally read the many books that hadn't yet been translated into Italian. He never became expert, but the flexibility of his brain is impressive. Most people find it extremely difficult to learn a new language at that age.

He followed any new development in geography or discovery of new plants and animals. He was mesmerized by maps. There is no evidence he ever journeyed farther than France—this was a time when most people never traveled farther than a day or two from their homes—but it was an electric era when people's notion of the geographical world was expanding rapidly. This was thanks in part to Italian merchants who were pressuring traders and sailors for exotic temptations, like precious spices, from the

Orient. After Christopher Columbus, financed by Spain, crossed the Atlantic Ocean and reached what turned out to be the "New World" in 1492, everyone's horizons were broadening fast. Leonardo himself was friends with Amerigo Vespucci, the Italian navigator who explored the New World from 1497 to 1504. (Vespucci was also intelligent enough to realize the continent was not part of Asia as Columbus believed, but a new one—which was later named after him.)

Practically the only facet of life that didn't interest Leonardo was current politics. Around him swirled intrigue, executions, invasions, violent changes in regime—none of which he wrote about. He tried to remain above it all, considering himself a "citizen of the world."

Yet there was no way to stop politics from intruding on his life. The French invaded Milan. Sforza, Leonardo's patron, was overthrown. In 1499, after eighteen years in Milan, Leonardo was forced to flee. He packed up his books, the precious notebooks, his collection of seeds (including lily and watermelon), and household items such as bowls and sheets—all in trunks to be carried by mules.

Together with Salai and Luca Pacioli, the forty-seven-year-old artist-scientist began to roam.

CHAPTER EIGHT

The Fabulous Notebooks

*A*T THE TIME Leonardo's mules were schlepping the notebooks around Italy, the pages were valuable only to their author. Today they are among the most precious things on the planet. The notebooks, the core obsession of Leonardo's life, are what place him among the giants of science, not specific discoveries he made or new inventions he created.

So what are they, exactly?

We call them "notebooks," but they are not bound like a typical notebook. Mostly they are loose sheets of paper casually gathered together and wrapped with different fabrics. Some pages are large. Others are only two or three inches square; these must be from the tiny blank notebooks he always kept tied to his belt.

Leonardo went out of his way to make the notebooks difficult for any other person to read—tremendously out of his way. The main roadblock is his famous mirror-image script. His tiny writing goes backward, reading from right to left. The drawings aren't backward, just the words.

What was he thinking?

Although he could draw with both hands, Leonardo remained left-handed. Was it simply easier or faster for him to write this way? Less smudging of the ink? Or was this eccentricity a function of his fear of scrutiny? Sometimes his work challenged church teachings. That could be dangerous. Was he worried that the notebooks could be used to incriminate him?

We know he lived in fear of having his ideas stolen and published. Although there is no evidence that anyone ever tried to steal his work, he dreaded that someone else would take credit for his beautiful brain flashes.

Sometimes he worried about "the evil nature of

men"—that bad guys would misuse his inventions. For example, he invented a diving suit but worried that people would use it to stay underwater long enough to drill holes and sink the ships of their enemies. He didn't trust many people.

He could also have been merely following common practice. Many astrologers and alchemists of the day wrote in code. The famous French seer Nostradamus, whose life overlapped with Leonardo's and who had run-ins with religious authorities, encoded all his predictions about the future.

Historians argue over Leonardo's reasons for being so baffling. In any case, much to a translator's exhaustion, the notebooks must be held up to a mirror to be read.

Even then, it's a challenge. Like other writers of his day, he used inconsistent spellings and abbreviations, no punctuation, and capitalization only rarely. On days when he must have been feeling especially secretive, he wrote in code.

And yet he was always addressing an imaginary readership—people who were brilliant, open to new ideas. Preferably geniuses. In the margins, he begged the reader to make sure his work got printed in book form—maybe, he hoped, after his death. So he wanted to be discovered and read. "I tell you . . . I teach you," he wrote frequently.

He boldly worked in ink—no revision. Lead pencils were uncommon in his day, anyway. When drawing the human body, he liked to work in red chalk, which he found good for conveying flesh. Getting paper was always a problem for him, and he obviously hated wasting it. He crammed every page with words and images. A page listing generous sums for Salai's clothes would be filled up with a recipe for a powder to make plaster models, as well as several dia-grams illustrating the play of light and shade. He mixed together shopping lists, thoughts for the day, tips for young artists, jokes whose humor hasn't lasted, and passages from borrowed library books.

The greatest hurdle for the reader is that his notes were not arranged in any logical order. He doesn't seem to have been a linear thinker; he jumps from insight to insight, sometimes with no apparent con-nection. Sometimes he contradicts himself. But because so many pages are lost and because Leonardo never dated his pages, it's impossible to know what his final thoughts on a subject were.

And—surprise!—he left everything unfinished. He worked as if he had all the time in the world, even though he was already elderly for his era.

The universally awe-inspiring aspect of the note-books is the sublime quality of the illustrations. These were no amateur doodles. No one could draw as well as Leonardo. Some think that no one has since, until computer-assisted draftsmanship was invented.

His text, although precise, witty, and often poet-ic, was there to explain the elegant artwork, not the other way around. He was of the "one picture is worth a thousand words" school, and no one who has ever seen one of his notebook pictures could argue against that. To Leonardo the key to everything was *saper vedere*—"knowing how to see." He wanted to be a sort of camera; he referred to "becoming like a mirror." The way he illustrated anything was always clear, dramatic. He observed, then recorded.

Whether he was studying the mysteries of flight; the relationship of the sun, moon, and stars; or the formation of fossils, he followed a pattern: recording ideas, doing experiments, and confirming or changing his ideas. It was a pattern revolutionary for its day— Leonardo was working his way toward the scientific method.

CHAPTER NINE

The Fabulous Notebooks, Part 2

THE CRUMBLING PAGES of Leonardo's notebooks are now five hundred years old. Ancient. How could they possibly be relevant to anything today?

Prepare to be surprised.

Leonardo was deeply interested in just about every area of science, but the three subjects he got the furthest on were anatomy, optics, and anything to do with water.

Medicine then was dominated by the twenty-two volumes of the ancient Greek Galen—who lived in the second century—and his theories about complexion and humors. The body had its own normal balance of four fluids, or "humors," as they were called: blood, phlegm, yellow bile, and black bile. Each of the four humors could be reduced to its basic qualities: hot, cold, wet, and dry. People's "complexions," or temperaments, could be classified the same way: sanguine (optimistic), phlegmatic (low in energy), choleric (easily angered), and melancholy (sad). So could organs—phlegm was associated with the brain, black bile with the spleen, and so forth.

Disease was a result of a person's "humors" getting out of balance for some reason. Diagnosis was a matter of doctors looking at the patient's urine and deciding which humor was out of balance, with bloodletting and vomiting as the usual recommended remedies. The heavens affected the humors, so astrology played a vital part in diagnosis. Almost any symptom—and cure—could be connected to the alignment of the planets on that particular day. There was no need to know the actual structure of an organ or how it functioned.

Leonardo, inspired by painting people from the outside, was determined to understand exactly what went on inside. There are plans in his notebooks for a whole book based on his drawings, to be called *On the Human Body*. Incredibly ambitious, it was to deal with how the body worked from the time it was a fetus right up until the moment of death. He wanted to explain the nervous system, the muscles and veins and capillaries, how the five senses worked, the flow of blood, each bone of the skeleton, every organ . . . everything. He wanted to *see*, in detail, how it all worked so he could *understand* how it all worked.

He had been able to dissect some animals, but he was itching to do the real thing—human dissections. In anatomy classes at medical schools, cutting into a human body—even a dead one—was considered repugnant. Human dissections were rare and generally done on the bodies of recently executed criminals. It was more important to read Hippocrates (the "father of medicine," born around 460 B.C.) and Galen (born in A.D. 129). Galen had dissected only dogs, pigs, and monkeys, yet his findings were applied to humans.

Historians disagree about exactly when Leonardo began dissecting human corpses. It's possible he may have started in the 1460s while still at Verrocchio's

workshop, to satisfy the master's demand for accuracy in painting. A famous professor of medicine, Marcantonio della Torre, may have smuggled Leonardo into a hospital in Florence and gotten him going on cadavers. (Some historians think Leonardo actually lived at the hospital for a time.)

After 1487, however, he became much more systematic and skilled in his study of human anatomy. He worked alone, by candlelight and only at night, to avoid prying eyes. In total, he dissected some thirty dead bodies, most of recently executed criminals or homeless beggars.

The more he learned, the more amazed he was at the intricacies of the human body: "I do not think that rough men, of bad habits and little intelligence, deserve such a fine instrument."

It is hard to exaggerate the creepiness of Leonardo's anatomy studies. There was no refrigeration or formaldehyde, so a corpse would have started to decay immediately. For his own sanity, Leonardo had to work as quickly as possible. But to get the information for his notebooks—the structure of the heart, for example, drawn from several different angles, and with the layers peeled back like the skin of an onion—he had to be on intimate terms with a corpse for as long as a week. Presumably he tried to schedule dissections for the colder winter months.

Here was an artist who didn't like getting paint under his fingernails; how did he deal with being up to his elbows in guts and gore? He described it in his notebooks as disturbing, "living through the night hours in the company of quartered"—cut into pieces—"and flayed corpses fearful to behold."

A serene person in general, Leonardo was cool, calm, and collected about witnessing what most people today could not bear to watch. Besides dissecting, he observed prisoners being tortured (he sketched their facial expressions) and executed. He did a quick but extremely realistic drawing of a nobleman's corpse dangling from a noose. People with amputated or deformed limbs—anyone who "broke the rules" of proportion—fascinated him.

Saws and scalpels were his tools, some of them his own inventions. After separating the organs, he washed them thoroughly in water and a solution of calcium oxide, or caustic lime. Now, how to get them to keep their shape long enough for him to draw everything from three different angles? He came up with his own method: he injected the organs with wax.

For eyeballs (notoriously squishy and hard to cut), he had the brainstorm of coating them with egg white first. Then he boiled them, to make them firmer, like hard-boiled eggs.

He didn't discard the bones and, in fact, was the first person to describe the human skeleton correctly. To discover how the parts of the body worked together, he would take a skeleton, insert copper wires where the muscles would go, and study how the contraction or relaxation of the wires caused different movements.

He once befriended a one-hundred-year-old man in a hospital, chatting for hours about his unusual longevity. Then the man died, and Leonardo immediately dissected his body to find out the cause of death. In describing the shriveled "artery that feeds the heart," he may have written the first description of arteriosclerosis (the hardening of the arteries) in history. A short time after dissecting the old man, he dissected the body of a two-year-old child. He noted all the differences between the healthy young organs and those he found in the body of the old man.

More than a century ahead of his time, Leonardo theorized that the heart was a thick muscle that pumped blood. The heart, according to Galen, was not even a muscle at all, but some unique tissue unlike anything else in the body. And in Leonardo's day, medical schools were teaching that blood came from two places—the liver as well as the heart.

Scientists then, and for centuries before, believed the valve to the heart to be a passive one. To test this, Leonardo created a glass model of the human aortic valve, inserting it into a cow's heart filled with water. He then poured water into the valve with bits of paper mixed in so that he could follow the movement of this new water. With this experiment, he demon-strated the correct motions of the valve opening and closing: he proved the valve was active.

Leonardo was the first person known to make a drawing of a baby inside a womb, although it wasn't entirely accurate. (The sacklike placenta was the wrong shape; it looked more like a cow placenta.) He was also one of the first to state that the mother and father have equal influence on an embryo—the belief of the day was that all characteristics of a baby came from the father.

Leonardo distilled his anatomy research into some 1,500 three-dimensional, multilayered drawings—again, he not only wanted to see but to record what he saw. The results were the first attempts at accurate depiction of human organs, muscles, and bones in history. His drawings have influenced medical textbooks to this day. There are cutaways and cross sections to show layers of an organ from various angles, as well as see-through images and sketches that portray as much motion as possible. His goal was to show the parts of the body in three dimensions. Five hundred years later, the drawings appear perfectly at home on the Internet.

Anatomy led to studies about vision and eyes, and Leonardo tried to break new ground in optics, although his knowledge was often primitive. In his day, many accepted Plato's belief that we see because our eyes project rays of light onto objects, then the rays are reflected back to the eye in an image. But Leonardo questioned Plato: how could this be true? If it were, wouldn't we see objects closer to us before we see ones farther away? But we don't. Our eyes take in a scene all at once.

Leonardo observed that when a knife stuck in a

table was made to vibrate, it gave the illusion of two knives. For Leonardo, this was more evidence that the eye receives images. It also told him that the eye finds it hard to distinguish images in quick succession.

As another test, Leonardo put a glass of water on a windowsill so that sunlight struck it. He observed that sunlight penetrated the glass and separated into different colors. His conclusion: the colors—the changes in the light—were a result of the water in the glass, not of what the eye was "projecting." In this and other experiments, he was influenced by the eleventh-century Arab philosopher Alhazen, who wrote a collection of essays on optics called *Opticae Thesaurus*.

Having mastered linear perspective as an artist also helped Leonardo develop his theories about vision. The principles of perspective set out by his old friend Alberti (who in turn stood on the shoulders of Brunelleschi) contained their own optical theories. But no artist was exploring vision as thoroughly as Leonardo was.

He kept revising his ideas until he came up with his own, simpler theory about light. From watching ripples made by stones tossed in a river, he leaped to the theory that light traveled in waves, and many believe he was the first person to realize this.

He was the first to write about the difference between peripheral (on the edge) and central vision. Also, he understood that a pair of eyes gathers information stereoscopically; the image seen by the left eye blends with the same image as seen by the right eye, allowing for depth perception. He discovered the reasons for farsightedness, and the principle behind the contact lens. He accurately listed the conditions under which the pupil of the eye changes in size. And he created a variety of optical devices, including what some believe was an early form of the telescope.

Leonardo had no great wealth to finance a laboratory; indeed, he brought the humblest of tools to his experiments. To test theories in optics and other fields, he used buckets, funnels, the eye of a needle, the ends of candles, metal boxes, sheets of paper pierced with holes, and the strings of a lute.

As with anatomy and optics, his notebook studies about water were breathtaking in their ambition. Pages had titles like "How to deal with rivers," "Of the flow and ebb," "Of what is water," and "Of the sea, which to many fools appears to be higher than the earth which forms its shore."

He studied all aspects of hydraulics (how to control water and use its power). He devised a scheme to divert rivers into canals and to reroute the Arno River, and invented various ingenious machines, among them drawings for an underwater vehicle resembling a submarine. He would spend hours on the banks of a river with his ear to a submerged tube, learning about how sound travels in water. Perhaps at some point he fell in—he even wrote swimming instructions and what to do if you were caught in a whirlpool.

Ripples and waves—how did they move? Leonardo dropped different-shaped objects into a bucket of water and saw that the ripples always formed in a circular pattern. He dropped in two objects at the same time to record the effect of merging ripples. His powers of observation were so keen that what he could see with the naked eye requires high-speed photography to record.

Watching waves—and depicting them in beautiful, curling drawings—led him into areas such as meteorology and geology. He seemed to have understood the principle of erosion, describing the way waves carry sand away and the way water "gnaws at mountains." He learned the effect of the moon on the tides, speculated about continent formation, and analyzed the nature of fossil shells found on mountaintops. One would think that, with his artistic eye, he would have been most interested in the beauty of shells and fossils—their forms and patterns. But he was after something else: to understand why they were there at all.

Leonardo grasped the principle that flooding water deposits layer upon layer of sediments (soil and sand), which turn into rock. At the same time, rivers erode rocks and carry their sediments to the sea, in a continuous cycle. He wrote, "The stratified stones of the mountains are all layers of clay, deposited one above the other by the various floods of the rivers."

In Leonardo's day, there were two theories about why fossils and shells were found in rocks on the tops of mountains. Some people believed the shells were carried there by the biblical Flood; others thought that these shells had grown in the rocks.

Leonardo pooh-poohed both hypotheses—such opinions "cannot exist in a brain of much reason." From his direct observation of shells and fossilized seaweed during walks in the Italian Alps, he came up with a third theory, one that is closer to the modern one. Shell fossils were once living organisms that had been buried at a time before the mountains were formed: "Where there is now raised land, there was once ocean." To Leonardo, as to modern paleontologists, fossils indicated that the history of the earth extended far beyond human records (such as the Bible)—"things are much more ancient than letters." Such theories would have offended a strict religious sensibility, as would his scrutiny of Bible passages for lack of scientific logic.

One day Leonardo wrote, "The sun does not move," in large letters on a page all by itself. We don't know exactly what he meant by this. He wasn't sure—he contradicted himself elsewhere in the notebooks. But was he beginning to question Ptolemy's ancient and still-popular view that the sun moved around the earth?

The notebooks covered a wealth of miscellaneous offerings—whatever interested Leonardo's butterfly mind. He tried to come up with a formula for making a synthetic material, something like plastic. It combined saffron, poppy dust, and whole lilies boiled together with eggs and glue.

Numerous themes, however, recur over and over: for example, the manipulation of nature through technology. The pages detailed all sorts of machines he designed with gears, cogwheels, screws, and pulleys.

He invented a bicycle that would have really worked. He borrowed freely from what others were doing at the time (as he did in all fields), but never without questioning the work or trying to improve it. Machines of all sorts fascinated him. In fact, Leonardo viewed the human body as a machine—the ultimate machine—capable of being understood by looking at its different parts.

Leonardo wanted to find new sources of energy. In an era when the main source of power was muscle (of men and horses), he looked at new ways of using water, wind, and steam. He constructed a device to measure the volume of steam coming off a certain quantity of boiling water. Some think he anticipated the invention of the steam engine hundreds of years later; at the very least, he understood the concept of steam as power. He also proposed using solar energy, trapped by mirrors he invented, to help out the textile industry.

And, of course, there was mastery of the air, his favorite and most obsessive dream. His notebooks played endlessly with this theme. He drew parachutes, gliders made from silk and reeds, wings with all combinations of strings and pulleys, and even a sort of helicopter with a whirling spiral of fabric above it. He puzzled about the best shape—should the flying object be a butterfly with four wings, a canoe with attachments, or more like a windmill's sails? Whatever the shape, his flying devices antici-pated sophisticated principles of aerodynamics, the branch of physics having to do with motion of the air.

His ideas were the results of years of observing birds and sketching them. "The bird is an instrument operating through mathematical laws," he believed—laws that *could* be figured out and applied to human flight. "As much pressure is exerted by the object against the air as by the air against the body," he wrote—a startling observation not fully developed until Isaac Newton in the seventeenth century. He observed bats and flies equally, and was a great admirer of the aerial techniques of bees. He borrowed ideas from everyone before him who had ever con-templated flying.

Historians agree that his contraptions were prob-ably not technically workable, but they disagree as to whether he actually made or tested any flying machine himself. If he did, we have no record of it.

Leonardo wasn't always right. For example, he

was intrigued by the study of physiognomy, the "science" of evaluating a person's character by his or her facial features. Like everyone in his time, he believed that a person's inner value was reflected on the outside. That is, good-looking people were virtuous, and ugly ones were bad. (Physiognomy was all the rage until completely debunked well after Leonardo's day.)

He believed in a sixth sense, "common sense," that ruled the other five senses. It was located, Leonardo said, in the center of the brain, "between sensation and memory." Like others of his day, he speculated (wrongly) about which sections of the brain related to distinct skills, and thought that nerves from the brain led directly to all body parts.

He was the first person to depict correctly the relationship of the small and large intestines, but in general he failed to grasp the digestive process. He was clueless about peristalsis (rhythmic contractions of the esophagus that propel food along), believing instead that food moved because of intestinal gas. He thought the purpose of the appendix was to relieve gas pressure. (Actually, it has no known purpose.)

His drawings of the reproductive system, based on Galen, were imaginative, but more inaccurate than accurate. His knowledge of women's anatomy lagged behind his knowledge of men's. Doctors at the time believed that a woman's uterus had seven chambers; Leonardo accepted this at first, though he soon realized it was false. But he never challenged the ancient belief that during pregnancy, a woman's menstrual blood travels up the blood vessels to the nipples to become the mother's breast milk.

Sometimes his theories were more poetry than science: "Tears come from the heart and not from the brain," he once wrote. He believed that children who were born out of love and desire would become intelligent and beautiful, while "unworthy" children would result from relationships of reluctance or scorn.

Partly because he was so far ahead of his time, his descriptions of experiments and theories were sometimes confusing. The proper scientific vocabulary simply didn't exist yet.

His desire to link things could lead him astray; he tried to make connections or parallels that didn't exist. Leonardo believed that, just as the heart inside our body pumps blood, an "underground" heart was the source of rivers, instead of the water cycle we know today.

He was always stretching to formulate all-encompassing principles—"everything travels in waves," "every natural phenomenon is produced by the shortest possible route," "motion is the principle of all life." Sometimes thinking big like this caused Leonardo to see patterns not always there. In his most famous drawing, the anatomically correct Vitruvian Man, he showed how the human body could be both a square and a circle. These shapes, he theorized, formed the basis of everything in the world. In this case, his theory was incorrect—another example of his seeing too much interconnection.

Sadly, he never gained mastery over mathematics, especially algebra. He even occasionally made basic mistakes in his arithmetic. He'd add up a list of numbers in his notebooks—and come up with the wrong total.

But in whatever he was investigating, Leonardo accepted nothing at face value. His theories were based on observation, documentation, and proof: "There is nothing more deceptive than to rely on your own opinion, without any other proof."

In the thousands upon thousands of pages in the notebooks, he was thinking like a scientist.

CHAPTER TEN

"I Have Wasted My Hours"

ROM 1500, WHEN Leonardo turned forty-eight, until just before his death in 1519, he was essentially homeless. Without even a country to ground him, he lived at times from day to day. A steady, sympathetic patron was once again proving elusive.

Traveling about with his small household made up of Salai and Luca Pacioli, he tried, within his limited means, to act the part of a refined aristocrat. He had the best horses. His servants were always well dressed, and he himself wore brocade and other fine fabrics.

In his trunks were precious cargo, forty books and his secret notebooks, except when he thought he might be in personal danger. Then he would leave them in a monastery, with someone he knew, for safe-keeping.

At least one observer noticed that he had grown "weary of the paintbrush." He often turned commissions over to his assistants. The reason to accept art commissions was to finance his experiments. He spent his days observing, measuring, dissecting, questioning, weighing, and analyzing—and cataloging it all in his notebooks.

In Florence, after the overthrow of the pleasure-loving, free-thinking Medici in 1494, the most powerful person was a teacher of religion named Girolamo Savonarola. In 1496, he staged a mass burning of what he considered immoral books and works of art. Luckily, only a few trusted friends knew about Leonardo's notebooks, or even of his interest in science. But many of his friends, labeled decadent, suffered under Savonarola.

For a while Leonardo designed weapons and fortresses for the most notorious of Italian warlords, Cesare Borgia, duke of Romagna. Duke Borgia was out to conquer all the city-states of Italy,

murdering anyone who stood in his way. Many historians have noted the irony here: Leonardo, who
despised war and called it *"bestialissima pazzia"*—
beastly madness—working for such brutal bosses.
But this was the highest-status work available to him.
He couldn't afford to turn it down, and he was gen-
uinely interested in devising anything mechanical. In
this case, the job gave him the liberty to explore
libraries and meet intellectuals all over Italy. He
became friends with Niccolò Machiavelli, the important Italian political writer and statesman.

Wherever he traveled, he drew gorgeous maps,
depicting geography with more detail and accuracy
than any previous cartographers. But after nine
months, Borgia's atrocities may have proved too
upsetting to Leonardo, who quit his post.

In 1504, he was invited to depict a Florentine
battle victory for the city's town hall. His archrival,
the twenty-nine-year-old Michelangelo, was invited
to paint another battle scene at the same time on
another wall in the same room.

The two geniuses had never gotten along.
Michelangelo showed no interest in science, which to
Leonardo meant his art was inferior. Michelangelo
had once publicly insulted the older artist for his

habit of leaving things unfinished. Leonardo, for possibly the first time in his life, had no instant comeback. He just blushed.

Leonardo put three years into his battle scene. He struggled to convey all the horrors of war. But while he was experimenting, trying to achieve the most brilliant colors possible, the paint on the wall ran and . . . well, he never actually finished the painting.

Leonardo also worked on several portraits during these years. The only one that survives is one he never titled. We call it the *Mona Lisa*. Leonardo seems to have had a special affection for the picture, for he never sold it, taking it with him on all of his subsequent travels.

Leonardo's worries would have been eased had he been able to count on a family inheritance. But when his father, Piero, died in 1504, Leonardo's meddling half brothers and sisters arranged to deprive their illegitimate sibling of any part of the estate. Then, a few years later, his favorite uncle, Francesco, died, specifically leaving everything to Leonardo. His siblings fought him on this as well. After a year in the courts, Leonardo prevailed and wound up with a small piece of land and money.

For a while he worked for King Louis XII of France, who was then living in Milan. Leonardo's job was building mechanical toys and other entertainments. Until he was an old man, Leonardo kept his love of toys, pranks, and riddles. Part of him remained childlike, playful, and open.

When asked to design a garden, Leonardo came up with a Renaissance Disneyland. It had musical instruments powered by water, a copper aviary for birds overhead, and miniature lakes with waterfalls to keep wine chilled. It even had playful sprays of water, "if one wanted to sprinkle the ladies' dresses for fun."

He and his intellectual friends gathered for dinners where they talked about science—and also fashioned paintings and sculptures entirely out of food. He met seventeen-year-old Francesco Melzi, the well-educated son of an aristocrat. Melzi was interested in everything Leonardo was doing and wanted a career as an artist. He joined Leonardo as a pupil and stayed with him for the rest of his life. At times, Leonardo lived on the Melzi family estate near Milan, sketching the dramatic countryside and designing improvements to his hosts' deluxe villa.

All this time, of course, Leonardo was continuing

to fill the notebooks. And he felt ever more pressure to put his work in some kind of order before he died. He was racing against time to arrange the information in one grand encyclopedia that people could read and learn from.

But the more he looked at the results of his years of investigation, the more dismayed he was at the chaos. The labor needed to sort out the bundles of unrelated papers was overwhelming.

So he put it off.

Organizing was a type of busywork that didn't really fit his personality. He reveled in flashes of insight. The actual cataloging of his insights would have cramped his style. And it wasn't as if the disorganization prevented him from carrying on. He had an extremely high tolerance for confusion—said to be a trait that many geniuses share.

Also, by 1515, no books could be printed in many regions without church permission, and he may have dreaded the process of censoring his notebooks in order to satisfy others.

Perhaps he lacked confidence in his ability to write proper scholarly books. He definitely wasn't up to writing effectively in Latin. He must have been nervous about his writing in general, because he sometimes asked friends to write important letters for him. At times in the notebooks, he worried about being laughed at. Perhaps he was plagued with depression, with bouts of sadness that sapped his energy. In any case, the notebooks remained note-books. "I have wasted my hours," he mourned.

In 1509, Leonardo's great friend Luca Pacioli died. From 1513 to 1516, Leonardo lived in Rome with the pope for a patron. Pope Leo X, the son of Lorenzo de' Medici, installed him in a comfortable suite of rooms in the Belvedere Palace inside the Vatican. Leonardo's duties were minimal, so he gladly occupied himself with science. The Vatican had exotic gardens that were perfect for his botanical studies.

Best of all, he was able to use his position to get church permission to do autopsies at San Spirito Hospital. He said they were necessary in the cause of improving his art. He continued doing dissections until an appalled assistant assigned by the pope accused him of conjuring spirits of the dead for evil purposes. Not wanting bad publicity, the pope banned Leonardo from the hospital.

Leonardo was bitter. By this time his eyesight was

fading, he wore glasses (of his own design), and he suffered from arthritis in at least one of his hands. There may have been other, unnamed ailments. He probably was treating himself; doctors knew so little that Leonardo always advised people to stay healthy and avoid these "destroyers of lives."

The newest pages in his notebooks were different. Now he was drawing violent end-of-the-world scenarios: huge uncontrollable surges of water, full of corpses and uprooted trees. The nightmarish images were perhaps his way of confronting his own death, his own doomed race against time.

CHAPTER ELEVEN

"I Will Continue"

IN 1517, LEONARDO made his last journey. To France.

King Francis I of France was obsessed with Italian Renaissance culture and art, and with Leonardo as well. The twenty-year-old new king had met the scientist-artist in 1515 when Leonardo had created a marvelous mechanical lion that actually walked a few steps. It may have been the world's first robot.

In France, Leonardo's pleasant new title was Premier Painter, Engineer, and Architect of the King. His chief duty was to chat with the king. It was a cushy job, including a generous salary as well as an elegant manor house called Clos Lucé near the king's summer palace in Amboise, about a hundred miles outside Paris. On the property were gardens, a fishing stream, vineyards, and a little house just for pigeons. Against the wall of his fully equipped studio, the *Mona Lisa* stayed propped.

Francis, a great supporter of the arts, considered Leonardo the smartest man alive and gave him the respect due a wise old grandfather. An underground tunnel connected his residence to Leonardo's, and Francis would drop in often, for long nights of stimulating conversation.

Here was the perfect patron—at last.

By this time, Leonardo's beard was long and white, and all his teeth were lost. His right hand seems to have gone numb, perhaps from a stroke. But he did not slow down. "I will continue," he wrote at age sixty-six.

He spent little time on painting or designing contraptions for warfare. He poured all his energy into science, trying to show how the universe operated under orderly laws. The world was rational, not magical; it could be understood.

"That science is the most useful whose results can be communicated," he reminded himself. He seemed aware that by keeping his work under wraps, he was failing to provide "shoulders" for others to stand on. But he could see that the task of sorting through thirty years of scientific notes was hopeless.

He decided to give it his best shot—to focus on organizing the information on water, painting, optics, and anatomy.

He worked in between visits from distinguished figures. One of his last visitors got a privileged viewing of presentable parts of the notebooks. The pages had to be turned for Leonardo, since his arm was now paralyzed. The visitor raved, "All these books . . . will be a source of pleasure and profit when they appear," even though, unfortunately, they were written in that "vulgar" tongue, Italian.

Leonardo listed chapter titles—some 120 just for anatomy alone—and gave himself deadlines. He scolded himself for not sticking to the task at hand: "The mind that engages in subjects of too great variety becomes confused and weakened."

At the same time, he was thinking more about his faith. Certain church practices had bothered him, especially the selling of indulgences—a way to receive pardon for one's sins in return for giving the church money. In 1517, the year Leonardo moved to France, Martin Luther condemned this same practice in Germany. Thus began the Protestant Reformation—and more than a century of violent wars over which religion would get a person to heaven.

Leonardo died at the very beginning of the movement. He never wrote about heaven. But before he died, he dictated that his last rites and burial be carried out according to Christian practice.

The end came in 1519, at age sixty-seven. As Melzi, his most loyal friend, nursed him, Leonardo died, no doubt while describing his symptoms and diagnosing his condition.

His will gave half of a vineyard to Salai, a fur coat to his housekeeper, and Uncle Francesco's property to his half brothers. Leonardo left everything else to Melzi—including the notebooks.

CHAPTER TWELVE

What Happened Next?

THE FATE OF the notebooks is not a happy story.

Francesco Melzi dutifully brought the thousands of notebook pages back to Italy. But as much as Melzi idolized his friend, he didn't fully comprehend the meaning of all that he'd inherited. He did hire two assistants to assemble Leonardo's theories on painting. However, the book of theories was not published until 1651.

Melzi tried to organize the rest of the notebooks for publication, but with little to show for it. Instead, he set aside a special room at his family's villa just for the notebooks, where invited visitors could view them. The visitors sometimes took pages with them as souvenirs—and so it began.

The notebooks gradually . . . disappeared.

After Melzi's death in 1570, it got worse. Having no idea of their importance, or not caring, his son Orazio stashed Leonardo's drawings and manuscripts randomly in chests in the attic. The Melzi family tutor made off with thirteen books for himself. Word spread that the family was giving sheets away or selling them cheaply. Strangers showed up at the Melzi front door. They weren't seeking scientific information. They were savvy art collectors, coveting the exquisite drawings.

Just as no one had valued Leonardo enough as a child to educate him, now no one valued his manuscripts enough to protect them. That tricky backward writing didn't help, either.

Nor did any biographer bother to do research on Leonardo's life until years after he had died. This explains why we have so few details about his life, especially his childhood—why there are so many *maybes* in this story.

Notebook pages were scattered in libraries and monasteries and private collections across Europe. One chunk ended up in Spain at the court of the king. In 1630, a sculptor named Pompeo Leoni decided he was up to the task of organizing Leonardo's work. First he wanted to pull out all the lessons on how to draw, and separate them from pages on science. So what he did was *cut and paste* Leonardo's pages to create two separate collections. Parts of both collections journeyed to Italy, then to France. Some science pages remained undiscovered until 1966, when they were found—accidentally—in Madrid.

Until 1883, when notebook extracts were finally published as a book, much of Leonardo's scientific work was unknown to the public. The book, however, had the misleading title of *The Literary Works of Leonardo da Vinci*—as if no one knew quite what to make of the material. In fact, the word *scientist* had been coined in 1834 in part to explain thinkers like Leonardo. The first exhibitions of Leonardo's scientific and technological work took place in the 1890s.

By the early twentieth century, people such as the Austrian psychiatrist Sigmund Freud were hailing Leonardo as "the first modern natural philosopher . . .

to investigate the secrets of nature, relying entirely on his observation and his own judgment."

Finally, official commissions were established to try to reconstruct the original arrangement of the manuscripts. Scholars sorted the notebook pages into ten books of what were called codices, now hungrily collected by museums. One codex, all about water, the only one in private hands, belongs to Bill Gates, founder of Microsoft and fan of Leonardo.

Much was lost, probably forever, due to carelessness, fires, floods, and wars. It is estimated that about half of the notes have surfaced (so far).

After Leonardo, discoveries about the natural world picked up speed. Big names were about to be emblazoned: Copernicus, Galileo, Newton. Many historians mark 1543—twenty-four years after Leonardo's death—as the start of the Scientific Revolution. The study of anatomy gradually became more respectable. Andreas Vesalius, a Flemish doctor, published *On the Structure of the Human Body* in 1543. For writing the first accurate book on anatomy, he is considered the father of modern medicine and biology.

That same year, Polish astronomer Nicolaus

Copernicus published his earth-shaking book, *On the Revolutions of Celestial Bodies.* The sun, not the earth, is the center around which planets revolve, declared Copernicus. Modern astronomy was on its way.

A hundred years before English doctor William Harvey published his discovery of the circulation of the blood in 1628, Leonardo had been investigating the body as a system of tubes, ducts, and valves, understanding that the heart moves blood.

Two hundred years before English scientist Isaac Newton published his famous Three Laws of Motion in 1687—his explanation for the scheme of the universe—Leonardo was exploring the reasons why objects fall and move the way they do. In his studies on flight, he observed how air resistance works. Newton said, "Objects at rest tend to remain at rest." Leonardo wrote, "Nothing moves, unless it is moved upon."

As for why the sky is blue, Leonardo understood that particles in the air somehow interact with light waves. In 1871, the English Lord Rayleigh worked out the exact reasons and got all the credit for the discovery.

Scottish geologist Charles Lyell, in the mid-1800s,

came to some of the same conclusions as Leonardo. Both of them theorized that Earth's characteristics—such as mountains and valleys—are the result of processes that took place over enormously long periods of time.

Four hundred fifty years before the Wright brothers flew in 1903, Leonardo was designing flying machines in every form he could conceive of, with the certainty that one day human beings would take to the air.

And so on, and so on, in and out of the centuries. It is an amusing game, with the advantage of hindsight, to find Leonardo everywhere.

It is possible to exaggerate his discoveries, or to regard him as an isolated miracle man. But he wasn't that isolated. Leonardo was able to draw from thinkers he admired. Sometimes all he did was point out the errors of his contemporaries. Sometimes he was wrong. And sometimes he leaped ahead in still mysterious ways as only geniuses are able to do. He was free to think what he pleased, with no university or school of thought stamped on his brain. But just the fact that he was delving into all these sciences is, for a man living in that long-ago world, stunning.

The big question is whether later scientists saw Leonardo's work and thus were able, as Newton said, to "see further." Because so much remained hidden away for so long, scientists after Leonardo carried on without his insights, unable to plant themselves atop his mighty shoulders and "see further."

Still, it is possible that Galileo, for example, was familiar with some of Leonardo's manuscripts. Also, we know that a later Dutch physicist had a brother who bought some Leonardo pages in London. In 1690, this physicist, named Christiaan Huygens, published his theory of the wavelike nature of light. Had he read about Leonardo's earlier work on the same theory? No way to tell.

In any case, other scientists after Leonardo, who arrived at similar conclusions, received the credit.

Leaving a paper trail—sharing knowledge with others—is a critical part of science. Leonardo himself wrote, "Avoid studies of which the result dies with the worker." But for many reasons, he never submit-ted his work for judgment by the outside world.

Still, it is hard to argue with the notion that, had the notebooks been published earlier, the history of science would have been completely different.

Anyone, not just hardcore scientists, who sees pages of a Leonardo notebook is spellbound. People want to run out and do an experiment or draw something from nature. Even today, scholars studying the notebooks are unveiling more and more connections between Leonardo's thoughts and current science. One historian called him "a man who wakes too early, while it is still dark and all around are sleeping."

Okay, he was a genius; this much is obvious. But does that explain Leonardo da Vinci? No. Someone so phenomenally gifted will always evade rational explanation.

True, he was like a surfer on a huge wave—the spirit of intellectual tolerance fostered by the Renaissance, the empowering access to information supplied by the new printing presses. Yet he always remained out of step: a left-handed, illegitimate, homosexual, antiwar vegetarian with extraordinary artistic talent. His outsider status took him on paths others couldn't even see.

So many tantalizing questions remain. If he had lived a century later, would he have been less of an outsider, more influential as part of the scientific mainstream? Would he *ever* have shared? Submitted his theories for review by peers? Published his work in a scientific journal?

In the final analysis, Leonardo can be credited not so much for specific discoveries as for a way of thinking. His devotion to scientific methods—investigating, observing, experimenting, and then forming conclusions—was revolutionary. He was open-minded, willing to toss out long-standing theories if he could disprove them.

Most intriguing of all is the question: What would Leonardo be doing if he were alive today?

LEONARDO'S NOTEBOOKS
AND WHERE THEY ARE NOW

LEONARDO'S MANUSCRIPTS TODAY are
nothing like the way they appeared and were grouped
together during his lifetime. Although many pages are
permanently lost, a chance still exists that priceless
pages could turn up—anywhere in the world. Be on the
lookout.

Today the notebooks are divided into ten different
assortments, as follows.

CODEX ARUNDEL

The name comes from Lord Arundel, an English collector
who pounced on Leonardo's work for King Charles I as
well as for himself. In this notebook—really just an
assortment of pages—Leonardo designs a complete new
city for King Francis I of France. "Let us have fountains
on every piazza," he remarks. Besides architecture, these
pages deal with geometry, weights, sound, and light. The
pages, some 238 of them, have been sliced from other
manuscripts and bound in leather. You can find them at
the British Library in London. But if you go to Turning
the Pages at The British Library, http://www.bl.uk/
collections/treasures/digitisation.html#leo, you can

come close to the sensation of physically turning the pages of this Leonardo notebook yourself.

CODEX ATLANTICUS

This notebook is the work of Pompeo Leoni, a six-teenth-century sculptor with nerve. Taking original Leonardo manuscripts from 1480 to 1518, Leoni used his own judgment in separating the scientific sketches from one, concerned with nature, anatomy, and the human figure. In this codex, made up of what he thought of as scientific materials, are some 1,119 sheets on astronomy, botany, zoology, geometry, and military engineering. Leoni titled his creation "Drawings of Machines, the Secret Arts, and Other Things by Leonardo da Vinci, collected by Pompeo Leoni." It has since been renamed the Atlanticus, and today the Biblioteca Ambrosiana in Milan is home to its twelve leather-bound volumes. Many (but not all) of what Leoni deemed to be the more artistic pages ended up in England, in the Royal Windsor collection.

CODEX TRIVULZIANUS

These pages detail Leonardo's ongoing efforts to edu-cate himself in literature, architecture, and other areas. The name comes from the codex's home—the Biblioteca Trivulziana at the Castello Sforzesco in Milan. At least seven out of the original sixty-two sheets are missing.

CODEX "ON THE FLIGHT OF BIRDS"

Held in the Biblioteca Reale of Turin, Italy, this collection from 1505 includes seventeen sheets of the original eighteen. It covers Leonardo's studies of birds, the mechanics of flight, air resistance, winds, and currents.

CODEX ASHBURNHAM

General Napoleon Bonaparte, in his expansion of French rule, made a point of amassing as much of Leonardo's work as he could; he later returned some of it to the original owners, but not this collection. Dating from about 1489-1492, these assorted drawings, bound in cardboard, remain in the Institut de France, in Paris.

CODICES OF THE INSTITUT DE FRANCE

Also at the Institut de France in Paris, these papers are bound together in various ways—by parchment, leather, or cardboard. Each of the twelve manuscripts is called by a letter of the alphabet, from A to M. The topics relate to Leonardo's usual interests—the flight of birds, hydraulics, optics, geometry, and military matters.

CODEX FORSTER

The Victoria and Albert Museum in London houses these manuscripts, bound in parchment, which focus on geometry and hydraulic machines.

CODEX LEICESTER

This codex was lost until 1690, when it was discovered in a sculptor's trunk. The Earl of Leicester bought it, and eventually it was purchased—for $30 million—by Bill Gates of Microsoft, at a 1995 auction. Its seventy-two linen sheets, bound in leather, detail all aspects of water and its movement; included is an illustration of what looks like a toilet. More information and pages to view are at http://www.amnh.org/exhibitions/codex/.

ROYAL WINDSOR FOLIOS

This notebook lives on in the Royal Collection of England's Windsor Castle. It includes the artistic drawings pulled by Italian sculptor Pompeo Leoni—some six hundred studies in human anatomy, horse anatomy, geography, and many other topics.

THE MADRID CODICES

These are the most recent discovery. At some point after their creation between 1503 and 1505, they were in the possession of Pompeo Leoni, and were then lost. Only in 1966 were they found once more, in the National Library of Madrid, Spain. The two manuscripts, bound in red leather, were named Madrid I (mostly on mechanics) and Madrid II (geometry).

A POSTSCRIPT

To better explain Leonardo da Vinci's contributions to science, this book has left out many details of his fabulous career as an artist. Visit your library for other books about him and his place in art history.

BIBLIOGRAPHY

BOOKS
(* books especially for young readers)

Bambach, Carmen C., ed. *Leonardo da Vinci: Master Draftsman.* New York: Metropolitan Museum of Art, 2003.

Bortolon, Liana. *The Life, Times, and Art of Leonardo.* New York: Crescent, 1965.

Bramly, Serge. *Leonardo: The Artist and the Man.* New York: Penguin, 1994. [For an assortment of reasons, writers have put a lot of imagination into telling the story of Leonardo da Vinci. I believe the most reliable facts are reported here.]

Brucker, Gene. *Florence, the Golden Age, 1138–1737.* Berkeley: University of California Press, 1998.

***Byrd, Robert.** *Leonardo: Beautiful Dreamer.* New York: Dutton, 2003.

Desmond, Michael, and Carlo Pedretti. *Leonardo da*

Vinci: The Codex Leicester—Notebook of a Genius. Sydney, Australia: Powerhouse Publishing, 2000.

Fairbrother, Trevor, and Chiyo Ishikawa. *Leonardo Lives: The Codex Leicester and Leonardo da Vinci's Legacy of Art and Science.* Seattle: Seattle Art Museum, 1997.

Freud, Sigmund, *Leonardo da Vinci: A Study in Psychosexuality.* New York: Random House, 1947.

Gelb, Michael J. *How to Think Like Leonardo da Vinci: Seven Steps to Genius Every Day.* New York: Random House, 1998.

Grant, Edward. *The Foundations of Modern Science in the Middle Ages: Their Religious, Institutional, and Intellectual Contexts.* Cambridge, United Kingdom: Cambridge University Press, 1996.

*Langley, Andrew. *Leonardo and His Times.* New York: Dorling Kindersley, 2000.

Leonardo da Vinci. *The Notebooks of Leonardo da Vinci*, compiled and edited from the original manuscripts by Jean Paul Richter (an unabridged edition of *The Literary Works of Leonardo da Vinci*, 1883), in two volumes. New York: Dover Publications, 1970.

Leonardo da Vinci. *The Notebooks of Leonardo da Vinci*, compiled and edited by Edward MacCurdy. Old Saybrook, Connecticut: Konecky & Konecky, 1939.

Lindberg, David C. *The Beginnings of Western Science*. Chicago: University of Chicago Press, 1992.

Lindberg, David C. *Theories of Vision from Al-Kindi to Kepler*. Chicago: University of Chicago Press, 1976.

Manchester, William. *A World Lit Only by Fire: The Medieval Mind and the Renaissance: Portrait of an Age*. Boston: Little, Brown, 1993.

Nuland, Sherwin B. *Leonardo da Vinci: A Penguin Life*. New York: Viking, 2000.

Rocke, Michael. *Forbidden Friendships: Homosexuality and Male Culture in Renaissance Florence*. New York: Oxford University Press, 1996.

Siraisi, Nancy G. *Medieval & Early Renaissance Medicine: An Introduction to Knowledge and Practice*. Chicago: University of Chicago Press, 1990.

White, Michael. *Leonardo: The First Scientist.* New York: St. Martin's, 2000.

WEB SITES
(Verified May 2008)

"Leonardo and the Engineers of the Renaissance," Institute and Museum of the History of Science, Florence, Italy: http://brunelleschi.imss.fi.it/ingrin (includes his robots and flying machines, pages from Codex Atlanticus and several other Notebooks)

"Leonardo da Vinci: A Man of Both Worlds": http://library.thinkquest.org/3044/index.html (includes 42 scientific drawings)

"Leonardo da Vinci, Master Draftsman," exhibit at the Metropolitan Museum, New York, 2003: http://www.metmuseum.org/special/Leonardo_Master_Draftsman/draftsman_tour.htm

"Leonardo da Vinci Notebook—Turning the Pages at the British Library": http://www.bl.uk/collections/treasures/digitisation.html#leo (pages from Codex Arundel)

"Leonardo da Vinci—Scientist—Inventor—Artist," Museum of Science, Boston: http://www.mos.org/leonardo/ (has classroom activities)

"Leonardo's Codex Leicester: A Masterpiece of Science," exhibit at the American Museum of Natural History, New York, 1997: http://www.amnh.org/exhibitions/codex/

"The Leonardo Museum in Vinci":
http://www.leonet.it/comuni/vincimus/invinmus.html

"Leonardo": National Museum of Science and Technology, Milan:
http://www.museoscienza.org/english/leonardo/ (includes one
hundred drawings of inventions and machines)

INDEX

abacus, 21
Adoration of the Magi (painting), 41
aerodynamics, 89
Alberti, Leon Battista, 33, 52, 65, 83
alchemy, 14
algebra, 92
Alhazen, 83
anatomy, 58, 64, 75, 81, 103, 108,
    artists' knowledge of, 28–29,
    Leonardo's study of, 9, 57, 74,
      80–81, 90–91, 118
    see also dissection
animals, 40
anonymous accusations, 35–36
anti-Semitism, 53
apprentices, 24, 26, 34
Arabic numbers, 64
Arabic scholars, 13–14, 46
Archimedes, 44, 65, 66
architecture, 53, 58, 115
Aristotelian logic, 46
Aristotle, 30, 46, 59, 66
army, career in, 23
Arno River, 85
art, career in, 24
arteriosclerosis, 80
artistic training, 24, 26,
    Leonardo's, 25, 27, 29, 31
arthritis, 100
astrology, 12, 14, 60–61, 75
astronomy, 9, 14, 56, 109, 116
autopsies, 99

Bacon, Roger, 46–47
Belvedere Palace, 99
Bible, 21
bicycle, invention of, 88
birds, 44, 89, 117
Black Death, 12, 25, 53, 54
    epidemic of 1348, 12
    cause, 54
blood, 81, 91
Bonaparte, Napoleon, 117
book publishing, 50

books, 21–22, 30, 43, 63, 65–66
    censorship and, 94, 98
    printed, 11, 21, 32
Borgia, Cesare, 94–95
botany, 9, 99, 116
brain structure, 90
Bramante, Donato, 52
British Museum, 115
bronze horse, statue, 51, 64
Brunelleschi, Filippo, 27, 83
bubonic plague, *see* Black Death
buchi della Verità, 35

Cardan, Fazio, 52
Caterina (mother of Leonardo), 18–19
censorship, 98
chemistry in artists' studios, 27
China, 13–14
Church, Catholic, 13, 22, 69, 98, 103–104
circulation of the blood, 81, 91, 109
cities, conditions, 11–12, 54
city planning, 54–55, 115
city-states, 24, 94
classical learning, 13–14, 21, 30, 44
Clos Lucé, 102
Codex Arundel, 115
Codex Ashburnham, 117
Codex Atlanticus, 116
Codex Forster, 117
Codex Leicester, 117
Codex "On the Flight of Birds," 117
Codex Trivulzianus, 116
Codices of the Institut de France, 117
Columbus, Christopher, 33, 67
comets, 33
contagion, 54
Copernicus, Nicolaus, 109

da Vinci, Francesco, 19–20, 96, 104
da Vinci, Leonardo
    appearance, 31, 41
    arrested, 35–39
    childhood, 18–19
    collections, 20

curiosity of, 32, 57
death of, 104
early biographies of, 106
household of, 62, 63, 67, 93, 97
isolation, 18, 19–20, 39, 112
lack of focus, 42–43, 87, 98, 103
need for privacy, 31, 39, 56
old age, 102
personality, 41, 42
secretiveness, 39, 65, 69–70, 112–13
sex life of, 38
da Vinci, Piero, 17–18, 23, 28, 37, 96
deformity, fascination with, 32
depression, 99
diet, 55–56
digestive process, 90
disease, 75
dissection, 28, 64, 76–80, 99
methods of, 78–80
Divina Proportione, 65
doctors, 12–13, 100
drawings, 20, 71, 72, 82, 100
techniques, 26–27, 29

Earth, position of, 14, 62, 63, 87, 109
education, 21–22, 30
Classical, lack of, 21, 48, 66
formal, 21
self-education, 22, 43, 44–47, 58, 116
encyclopedias, 46, 59, 98
energy, search for new sources of, 88
engineer-architect, 48, 62
erosion, 85–86
Euclid, 65
experimentation, 9, 47, 57–58
Leonardo's experiments, 47, 81,
82–83, 84, 85, 88
explorers, 66–67
eye, structure of, 52, 80, 82, 84

famine, 12
Fazio, Cardan, 52
Feast of Paradise, 60
flight, study of, 21, 43–44, 88–89, 109,
110, 117
Florence, 17–18, 24, 25–26, 31, 38, 43, 94
Florentine painters' guild, 34

flying machines, 89
fossils, 86–87
theories of, 87
France, 66, 97, 101
Francis I, King of France, 101, 102
Freud, Sigmund, 107

Galen, 74–75, 76, 81, 90
Galileo, 111
Gates, Bill, 108, 118
geography, 66–67, 118
geology, 9, 110
geometry, 115, 116, 117, 118
Giotto, 48
glasses, 100
Greece, 13–14
Gutenberg, Johannes, 21, 32

Harvey, William, 109
health, rules for, 55
heart, theories of, 81, 91
helicopter, invention of, 89
heredity, theory of, 81
Hippocrates, 76
history of science, 9
homosexuality, 36, 37, 38
humors, theory of, 75
Huygens, Christian, 111
hydraulics, 84–85, 117

Icarus, 44
illegitimacy, 18, 22, 23, 112
income, 48, 62, 84, 96, 102
indulgences, 104
influence of Leonardo on other
scientists, 9, 111–12
inheritance, 96
inventions, 43
Islamic scholars, 14
Italian, as "vulgar tongue," 21, 103
Italy, 24

jokes, 31, 72

knowledge, unifying theories and
principles of, 57–58, 91–92
Last Supper, The (painting), 8, 63–64

Ptolemy, 63, 87

rats, 53
Rayleigh, Lord, 109
religious beliefs, Leonardo's, 22, 87,
  103–104
Renaissance, 14–15, 33, 112
reproductive system, 81, 90
robot, 101
Roman numerals, 21, 64
Rome, 13–14, 99
rose water perfume, 53
Royal Windsor Folios, 118

Salai, 63, 67, 71, 93, 104
sanitation, 11, 12, 54
Savonarola, Girolamo, 94
scholars, 33, 43
science, state of in Renaissance, 13–14
      Leonardo's education in, 30, 32, 40
      relationship to art, 27, 33
scientia, 9
scientific ideas, origins, 8
scientific method, 15, 47, 59, 73, 92, 113
Scientific Revolution of 1543, 108
scientific vocabulary, 91
scientist, Leonardo's development as, 57,
  102–103
"scientist" as a term, 9, 107
self-education, 22, 43, 44–47, 58
Sforza, Duke Ludovico, 51, 53, 60, 62
      job application to, 51–52
      overthrown, 67
Sistine Chapel, 48
sixth sense, 90
skeletons, 80
solar eclipses, 56
solar energy, 88
St. Peter's Basilica in Rome, 52
steam power, 88
submarines, 47, 85

telescope, 84
tides, 85
toilets, 118
Torre, Marcantonio della, 78
torture, 37, 79

Toscanelli, Paolo, 32–33
trade, 23
travel, 66

unfinished projects, 41, 59, 64, 72, 96,
  98
universal theories, 57–58, 91–92
universities, 12, 22, 32, 34, 50, 63
University of Pavia, 51

Vatican, 99
vegetarian, 55
Verrocchio, Andrea del, 24, 26, 28,
  34, 47, 76–77
Vesalius, Andreas, 108
Vespucci, Amerigo, 67
Vinci (town), 17, 20
vision, 83, 84
Vitruvian Man, 92

warfare, 13, 47, 95, 117
water, study of, 19, 21, 47, 74, 84–86,
  108, 118
waves, movement of, 85
weapons, 47, 51, 94, 116
wings, 89
Women, position of in society, 13, 38
      anatomy of, 81, 90–91
Wright brothers, 110

zodiac, 62
zoology, 9

Latin, 21, 48, 66, 99
Laws of Motion, 108
left-handedness, 22, 69, 112
Leo X, Pope, 99
Leoni, Pompeo, 107, 116, 118
lever, invention of, 44
libraries, 43, 51, 63
life expectancy, 11–12
light, theories of, 46, 82–83, 109, 111, 115
linear perspective, 26–27, 83
literacy, 11, 32
Literary Works of Leonardo da Vinci, The, 107
Louis XII, King of France, 97
Luther, Martin, 104
Lyell, Charles, 109–10

Machiavelli, Niccolò, 95
Madrid Codices, The, 118
manuscripts, 11
maps, 66, 95
Masque of the Planets, 60, 61–62
mathematics, 21, 27, 47
 Leonardo's limited knowledge of, 64–65, 92
mechanical devices, 47, 85, 87, 88, 97, 101
medical training, 12, 28
Medici, 25–26, 31, 34, 35
Medici, Lorenzo de' (the Magnificent), 25, 36, 37, 48–49, 94, 99
medicine, medieval, 12–13
 Renaissance, 74–75, 100, 108
medieval worldview, 9
Melzi, Francesco, 97, 104, 105–106
Melzi, Orazio, 106
Michelangelo, 95–96
Microsoft, 107, 118
Middle Ages, life in, 11–13
Milan, 50, 53, 56, 67
military engineer, 53
mirror-image script, 69–71
Mona Lisa (painting), 8, 96, 102
moon, 46
mortality rates, 11–12, 13
musical ability, 31, 41

natural philosopher (term), 9

nature, direct study of, 9, 20, 21, 58
Newton, Isaac, 8, 89, 109
"New World," 67
Nostradamus, 70
notary, 17
notebooks, Leonardo's, 50, 56–59, 65, 67, 68–92, 94, 100, 104
 arrangement of, 72, 98
 described, 68–69, 71, 103
 fate of, 105–108, 115
 publication, 105, 107, 111
 readership of, 71
 see also under individual codex names

observation skills, 73
Office of the Night, 36
On Floating Bodies, 66
On the Revolutions of Celestial Bodies, 109
On the Structure of the Human Body, 108
Opticae Thesaurus, 83
optics, 52, 65, 74, 82–84, 117
outer space, 60

Pacioli, Luca, 64–65, 67, 93, 99
pageants, designs for, 56, 60, 61–62
painting
 Leonardo's attitude toward, 42, 47, 51–52, 94
 methods, 26, 64
 theories on, 105
paintings, Leonardo's, 8, 28
 number of, 41
 see also individual paintings
paleontology, 9, 87
paper, 20, 71
patronage, 48, 93, 102
peasants, living conditions, 11–12
peripheral vision, 84
physiognomy, 14, 90
plague, *see* Black Death
planets, 14, 62
Plato, 30, 44, 65, 82
Pliny, 66
politics, Leonardo's disinterest in, 67
pranks, 30, 97
Protestant Reformation, 104
pseudosciences, 14